Travellers' Serbo

David Ellis is Director of the
and co-author of a number o

Eugenia Spong was born in Dubrovnik and now lives in
London where she works as an interpreter

Dr John Baldwin is Lecturer in Phonetics at
University College, London

Other titles in the series

Travellers' **Serbo-Croat**
for Yugoslavia

D. L. Ellis, E. Spong

Pronunciation **Dr J. Baldwin**

Pan Books London and Sydney

Whilst the advice and information in this book is believed to be
true and accurate at the time of going to press, neither the
authors nor the publisher can accept any legal responsibility or
liability for any errors or omissions that may be made

The publishers would like to thank the Yugoslav National Tourist
Office for their help during the preparation of this book

First published 1981 by Pan Books Ltd,
Cavaye Place, London SW10 9PG
2 3 4 5 6 7 8 9
© D. L. Ellis and E. Spong 1981
ISBN 0 330 26381 1
Printed and bound in Great Britain by
Hunt Barnard Printing Ltd, Aylesbury, Bucks

This book is sold subject to the condition that it
shall not, by way of trade or otherwise, be lent, re-sold,
hired out, or otherwise circulated without the publisher's prior
consent in any form of binding or cover other than that in which
it is published and without a similar condition including this
condition being imposed on the subsequent purchaser

Contents

Using the phrase book

- This phrase book is designed to help you get by in Yugoslavia, to get what you want or need. It concentrates on the simplest but most effective way you can express these needs in an unfamiliar language.
- Yugoslavia is made up of six socialist republics and two socialist autonomous provinces within the Republic of Serbia. It is a country inhabited by six nations and several nationalities all of whose languages enjoy equal recognition. The most widely spoken language is Serbo-Croat, followed by Slovenian and Macedonian. Serbo-Croat is spoken in Bosnia-Herzegovina, Montenegro, Croatia and Serbia.
- The CONTENTS on p. 5 gives you a good idea of which section to consult for the phrase you need.
- The INDEX on p. 151 gives more detailed information about where to look for your phrase.
- When you have found the right page you will be given:
  either – the exact phrase
  or   – help in making up a suitable sentence
  and – help to get the pronunciation right
- The English sentences in **bold type** will be useful for you in a variety of different situations, so they are worth learning by heart. (See also DO IT YOURSELF, p. 143.)
- Whenever possible you will find help in understanding what Yugoslav are saying to *you*, in reply to your questions.
- If you want to practise the basic nuts and bolts of the language further, look at the DO IT YOURSELF section starting on p. 143.
- Note especially these three sections:
  Everyday expressions p. 12
  Shop talk p. 56
  Public notices p. 121
  You are sure to want to refer to them most frequently.
- Once abroad, remember to make good use of the local tourist offices (see p. 26).
  UK address:
  Yugoslav National Tourist Office
  143 Regent Street
  London W1

A note on the pronunciation system

It is usual in phrase books for there to be a pronunciation section, which tries to teach English-speaking tourists how to pronounce correctly the language of the country they are visiting. Such attempts are based on the argument that correct pronunciation is essential for comprehension. The system in this book, however, is founded on three quite different assumptions: firstly, that it is not possible to describe in print the sounds of a foreign language in such a way that the English speaker with no phonetic training will produce them accurately, or even intelligibly; secondly, that perfect pronunciation is not essential for communication and lastly that the average visitor abroad is more interested in achieving successful communication than in learning how to pronounce new speech sounds. Observation and experience have shown these assumptions to be justified. The most important characteristic of the present system, therefore, is that it makes no attempt whatsoever to teach the sounds of the other language, but uses instead the nearest English sounds to them. The sentences transcribed for pronunciation are designed to be read as naturally as possible, as if they were ordinary English (of a generally south-eastern variety), and with no attempt to make the words sound 'foreign'. In this way you will sound quite English but you will at the same time be understood. Practice always helps performance and it is a good idea to rehearse out loud any of the sentences you know you are going to need. When you come to the point of using them, say them with conviction.

In Serbo-Croat, it is important to stress or emphasize the syllables in *italics*, just as you would if we were to take as an English example: Little Jack Horner s*a*t in the c*o*rner. Here we have ten syllables but only four stresses.

Of course you may enjoy trying to pronounce a foreign language as well as possible, and the present system is a good way to start. However, since it uses only the sounds of English, you will very soon need to depart from it as you begin to imitate the sounds you hear the native speaker produce and relate them to the spelling of the other language.

For interest, below you will find the characters of the Cyrillic alphabet which you will probably not need but which is used throughout Yugoslavia – except in Slovenia and Croatia where the Roman alphabet is in use. The columns on the left show the printed capital and small letters, and the one on the right the corresponding letter in the Roman alphabet (as used in this book).

А	а	a	Г	г	g	О	о	o
Б	б	b	Х	х	h	П	п	p
Ц	ц	c	И	и	i	Р	р	r
Ч	ч	č	Ј	ј	j	С	с	s
Ћ	ћ	ć	К	к	k	Ш	ш	š
Д	д	d	Л	л	l	Т	т	t
Џ	џ	dž	Љ	љ	lj	У	у	u
Ђ	ђ	dj	М	м	m	В	в	v
Е	е	e	Н	н	n	З	з	z
Ф	ф	f	Њ	њ	nj	Ж	ж	ž

Dobra zabava!
John Baldwin, 1980

For instance, below you will find the transcription of the Cyrillic alphabet which you will probably not need but which passed through out Yugoslavia – except in Slovenia and Croatia where the Roman alphabet is in use. The columns on the left show the printed capital and small letters, and the one on the right the corresponding letter in the Roman alphabet I use in this book.

Dobra zabava!
Jože Dežman, 1985

Republics and main towns

Italy
Austria
Ljubljana
SLOVENIJA
Hungary
Pula
Rijeka
Zagreb
HRVATSKA (CROATIA)
Zadar
Romania
Sibenik
Split
BOSNA I
Sarajevo
Beograd
HERCEGOVINA
SRBIJA
Dubrovnik
CRNA GORA
(MONTENEGRO)
Titograd
Bar
Skopje
MAKEDONIJA
Bulgaria
Albania
Greece

Everyday expressions

[*See also 'Shop talk', p. 56*]

Hello (informal)	**Zdravo**
	zdra-fo
Good morning	**Dobro jutro**
	dob-ro yootro
Good day (hello)	**Dobar dan**
	dob-ar dun
Good night	**Laku noć**
	la-koo noch
Goodbye	**Zbogom**
	zbog-om
See you later	**Dovidjenja**
	doveejen-ya
Yes	**Da**
	da
Please	**Molim**
	mol-im
Yes, please	**Da, molim**
	da mol-im
Great!	**Divno!**
	deev-no
Thank you	**Hvala vam**
	fa-la vum
Thank you very much	**Puno vam hvala**
	poono vum fa-la
That's right	**Točno**
	toch-no
No	**Ne**
	neh
No, thank you	**Ne, hvala**
	neh fa-la
I disagree	**Ne slažem se**
	neh sla-shem seh
Excuse me ⎤ Sorry ⎦	**Oprostite/pardon**
	oprost-eet-eh/par-don
Don't mention it ⎤ That's OK ⎦	**Molim**
	mol-im
That's good ⎤ I like it ⎦	**Dobro je**
	dob-ro jeh

That's no good ⎤ I don't like it ⎦	**Nije dobro** nee-yeh dob-ro
I know	**Znam** znum
I don't know	**Ne znam** neh znum
It doesn't matter	**Ne smeta** neh smeh-ta
Where's the toilet, please?	**Gdje je toaleta, molim?** gd-yeh yeh twa-leh-ta mol-im
How much is that? [*point*]	**Koliko to košta?** kol-eeko toh koshta
Is the service included?	**Da li je servis uračunat?** da lee yeh sairvis oora-choo-nat
Do you speak English?	**Govorite li engleski?** gov-oree-teh lee en-glesky
I'm sorry . . .	**Žao mi je . . .** sha-o mee yeh . . .
I don't speak Serbo-Croat	**ne govorim srpsko-hrvatski** neh gov-oreem serpsko-hervatsky
I only speak a little Serbo-Croat	**govorim samo malo srpsko-hrvatski** gov-oreem sa-mo mai-lo serpsko-hervatsky
I don't understand	**ne razumjem** neh razoom-yem
Please can you . . .	**Molim vas, možete li . . .** mol-im vus mosh-et-eh lee . . .
repeat that?	**to ponoviti?** toh pono-veetee
speak more slowly?	**govoriti polaganije?** gov-oreetee pola-gan-ee-yeh
write it down?	**napisati?** napeesat-ee
What is this called in Serbo-Croat? [*point*].	**Kako se zove ovo u srpsko-hrvatskom jeziku?** ka-ko seh zhov-eh ov-o oo serp sko hervat-skom yez-eekoo

Crossing the border

ESSENTIAL INFORMATION

- Don't waste time just before you leave rehearsing what you're going to say to the border officials – the chances are that you won't have to say anything at all, especially if you travel by air.
- It's more useful to check that you have your documents handy for the journey: passport, tickets, money, travellers' cheques, insurance documents, driving licence and car registration documents.
- Look out for these signs:
  CARINARNICA (customs)
  GRANICA (border)
  GRANIČNA MILICIJA (frontier police)
  [For further signs and notices, see p. 121]
- You may be asked routine questions by the customs officials [see below]. If you have to give personal details see 'Meeting people', p. 16. The other important answer to know is 'Nothing': Ništa (neesh-ta).

ROUTINE QUESTIONS

Passport?	**Pasoš?**
	pas-osh
Insurance?	**Osiguranje?**
	oseegoo-ran-yeh
Registration document? (logbook)	**Saobraćajnu knjižicu**
	sa-obracha-eenoo kn-yee-shee-tsoo
Ticket, please	**Kartu, molim**
	kartoo mol-im
Have you anything to declare?	**Imate li išta za prijaviti?**
	eemat-eh lee eesh-ta za pree-ya-veet-ee
Where are you going?	**Gdje idete?**
	gd-yeh eedet-eh
How long are you staying?	**Koliko ćete se zadrzati?**
	kol-eeko chet-eh seh zader-shatee
Where have you come from?	**Odakle dolazite?**
	odak-leh dolaz-eeteh

You may also have to fill in forms which ask for:

surname	**prezime**
first name	**ime**
place of birth	**mjesto rodjenja**
date of birth	**datum rodjenja**
address	**adresa**
nationality	**narodnost**
profession	**zanimanje**
passport number	**broj pasoša**
issued at	**izdan u**
signature	**potpis**

Meeting people

[See also 'Everyday expressions', p. 12]

Breaking the ice

Hello	**Dobar dan**
	dob-ar dun
Good morning	**Dobro jutro**
	dob-ro yootro
How are you?	**Kako ste?**
	ka-ko steh
Pleased to meet you	**Drago mi je upoznati vas**
	dra-go mee yeh oopozna-tee vus
I am here . . .	**Ovdje sam . . .**
	ovd-yeh sum . . .
on holiday	**na odmoru**
	na odmoroo
on business	**poslovno**
	poslov-no
Can I offer you . . .	**Mogu li vam ponuditi . . .**
	mog-oo lee vum pon-oodeetee . . .
a drink?	**nešto za piti?**
	nesh-to za peetee
a cigarette?	**cigaretu?**
	tseega-reh-too
a cigar?	**cigar?**
	tseegar
Are you staying long?	**Hoćete li se zadržati dugo?**
	hoch-et-eh lee seh zader-shatee doogo

Name

What's your name?	**Kako se zovete?**
	ka-ko seh zov-et-eh
My name is . . .	**Ja se zovem . . .**
	ya seh zov-em . . .

Family

Are you married?	**Da li ste oženjen/udata*?**
	da lee steh *o*shen-yen/*oo*da-ta?
I am . . .	**Ja sam . . .**
	ya sum . . .
married	**oženjen/udata***
	*o*shen-yen/*oo*da-ta
single	**neoženjen/neudata***
	neh-*o*shen-yen/neh-*oo*d-ata
This is . . .	**Ovo je . . .**
	*o*v-o yeh . . .
my wife	**moja žena**
	moya shen-a
my husband	**moj muž**
	moy moosh
my son	**moj sin**
	moy seen
my daughter	**moja kćerka**
	moya ch*ai*rka
my (boy) friend	**moj mladić**
	moy mlad-eech
my (girl) friend	**moja djevojka**
	moya dee-yev-oy-ka
my (male) colleague	**moj kolega**
	moy kol-ega
my (female) colleague	**moja kolegica**
	moya kol-eg-eetsa
Do you have any children?	**Imate li djece?**
	*ee*mat-eh lee dee-yets-eh
I have . . .	**Imam . . .**
	*ee*m-am . . .
one daughter	**jednu kćerku**
	yed-noo ch*ai*r-koo
one son	**jednog sina**
	yed-nog s*ee*na
two daughters	**dvije kćerke**
	dv*ee*-yeh ch*ai*r-keh
three sons	**tri sina**
	tree s*ee*na

*For men use the first alternative, for women the second

No, I haven't any children	**Nemam djece**
	nem-am dee-yets-eh

Where you live

Are you . . .	**Jeste li . . .**
	yest-eh lee . . .
Italian?	**Talijan/Talijanka*?**
	talee-yan/talee-yanka
Swiss?	**Švajcarac/Švajcarka*?**
	shvay-tsa-rats/shvay-tsarka
Yugoslav?	**Yugoslaven/Yugoslavenka*?**
	yoogo-sla-ven/
	yoogo-sla-venka
I am . . .	**Ja sam . . .**
	ya sum . . .
American	**Amerikanac/Amerikanka***
	amerika-nats/amerikanka
English	**Englez/Engleskinja***
	en-glez/en-glez-keen-ya

[*For other nationalities, see p. 136*]

I am . . .	**Ja sam . . .**
	ya sum . . .
from London	**iz Londona**
	eez lond-ona
from England	**iz Engleske**
	eez en-gles-keh
from the north	**sa sjevera**
	sa see-ev-era
from the south	**sa juga**
	sa yooga
from the east	**sa istoka**
	sa eest-oka
from the west	**sa zapada**
	sa zapada
from the centre	**iz centra**

[*For other countries, see p. 134*] eez tsen-tra

*For men use the first alternative, for women the second

For the businessman and woman

I work for . . . (firm's name)	**Ja radim za . . .** ya rad-eem za . . .
I have an appointment with . . .	**Imam sastanak sa . . .** eem-am sast-anak sa . . .
May I speak to . . . ?	**Mogu li govoriti sa . . . ?** mog-oo lee gov-oree-tee sa . . .
This is my card	**Ovo je moja posjetnica** ov-o yeh moya pos-yet-nitsa
I'm sorry, I'm late	**Oprostite, zakasnio sam** oprost-eet-eh zakas-nee-o sum
Can I fix another appointment?	**Mogu li ugovoriti drugi sastanak?** mog-oo lee oogovo-reetee droog-ee sast-anak
I'm staying . . .	**Ja sam odseo/odsjela* . . .** ya sum ods-yeh-o/ods-yel-a . . .
at the hotel (Belgrade)	**u hotel Beograd?** oo hotel beh-ograd
in (Rebulic) square	**na trgu (Republike)** na tergoo (repub-leeke)

*For men use the first alternative, for women the second

Asking the way

ESSENTIAL INFORMATION

● Keep a look out for all these place names as you will find them on shops, maps and notices.

WHAT TO SAY

Excuse me, please	**Oprostite, molim**
	oprost-eet-eh mol-im
Which is the way . . .	**Koji je put . . .**
	koyee yeh poot . . .
to Belgrade?	**za Beograd?**
	za beh-ograd
to (Republic) street?	**za ulicu (Republike)?**
	za ooleetsoo (repoob-leekeh)
to the Hotel Lapad?	**za Hotel Lapad?**
	za hotel lap-ad
to the airport?	**za aerodrom?**
	za ah-airodrom
to the beach?	**za plažu?**
	za plash-oo
to the bus station?	**za autobusnu stanicu?**
	za ah-ooto-boosnoo stan-eetsoo
to the historic site?	**za historijsko mjesto?**
	za heestoree-sko m-yesto
to the market?	**za tržnicu?**
	za ter-shnee-tsoo
to the police station?	**za miliciju?**
	za meel-eets-yoo
to the port?	**za luku?**
	za loo-koo
to the post office?	**za poštu?**
	za posh-too
to the railway station?	**za željezničku stanicu?**
	za shel-yezneech-koo stan-eetsoo
to the sports stadium?	**za športski stadion?**
	za shport-skee stad-ee-on

to the tourist information office	**za turistički ured?** za toorist-eech-kee oo-red
to the town centre?	**za centar grada?** za tsen-tar gra-da
to the town hall?	**za gradsku općinu?** za grat-skoo op-chee-noo
Excuse me, please	**Oprostite, molim** oprost-eet-eh mol-im
Is there . . . near by?	**Ima li ovdje blizu . . .?** eema lee ovd-yeh blee-zoo . . .
an art gallery?	**umjetnička galerija?** oomyet-neech-ka galair-eeya
a baker's	**pekarna** pek-arna
a bank	**banka** ban-ka
a botanical garden	**botanički vrt** bot-aneech-kee vert
a bus stop	**autobusna stanica** ah-ooto-boosna stan-eetsa
a butcher's	**mesarnica** mesar-neetsa
a café	**kavana** kava-na
a cake shop	**slastičarna** slastee-charna
a campsite	**autokamp** ah-ooto-kamp
a car park	**parkiralište** par-kee-ral-eeshteh
a change bureau	**mjenjačnica** m-hyen-yach-neetsa
a chemist's	**apoteka** apotek-ah
a church	**crkva** tserk-va
a cinema	**kino** keeno
a concert hall	**dvorana za koncerte** dvora-na za kon-tsairteh
a delicatessen	**delikatesna radnja** delikates-na radn-ya

Is there . . . near by?	**Ima li ovdje blizu . . .?**
	eema lee ovd-yeh blee-zoo . . .
a dentist's	**zubar**
	zoobar
a department store	**robna kuća**
	robna koocha
a disco	**disko klub**
	disko-cloob
a doctor's surgery	**liječnička ordinacija**
	lee-yech-neechka ordeen-atsee-ya
a dry cleaner's	**kemijska čistiona**
	kem-eeska cheest-yona
a fishmonger's	**ribarnica**
	reebar-neetsa
a garage (for repairs)	**garaža**
	gara-sha
a hairdresser's	**frizer**
	friz-air
a greengrocer's	**voćarna**
	voch-arna
a grocer's	**dućan mješovite robe**
	doochan m-yesh-oveeteh robeh
a hardware shop	**željezara**
	shel-yez-ara
a hospital	**bolnica**
	bol-nitsa
a hotel	**hotel**
	hotel
an ice-cream parlour	**slastičarna**
	slasti-charna
a laundry	**praonica**
	pra-on-eetsa
a museum	**muzej**
	moo-zay
a newsagent's	**prodavaona novina**
	prodava-ona novee-na
a night club	**noćni lokal**
	nochni lok-al
a park	**park**
	park
a petrol station	**benzinska stanica**
	benzeen-ska stan-eetsa

a post box	**poštanski sandučić**
	poshtan-skee sand-*oo*chitch
a public garden	**park**
	park
a restaurant	**restoran**
	rest-oran
a snack bar	**snek bar**
	snack bar
a sports ground	**športsko igralište**
	shport-sko eegra-*lee*shteh
a supermarket	**supermarket/robna kuća**
	supermarket/r*o*bna k*oo*cha
a swimming pool	**bazen**
	b*a*z-en
a taxi stand	**stajalište taksija**
	st*a*-yaleesh-teh t*a*k-see-ya
a telephone	**telefon**
	telephon
a theatre	**kazalište**
	k*a*z-aleeshteh
a tobacconist's	**trafika**
	tr*a*f-eeka
a toilet	**toaleta**
	tw*a*-leh-ta
a travel agent's	**putna agencija**
	p*oo*tna agents*e*e-ya
a youth hostel	**omladinski dom**
	*o*mlad-een-skee dom
a zoo	**zoološki vrt**
	z*oo*-losh-kee v*e*rt.

[*continued over*]

DIRECTIONS

- Asking where a place is, or if a place is near by, is one thing; making sense of the answer is another.
- Here are some of the most important key directions and replies.

Left	**Lijevo**
	lee-yev-o
Right	**Desno**
	desno
Straight on	**Ravno**
	ravno
There	**Tamo**
	tamo
First left/right	**Prva na lijevo/na desno**
	perva na lee-yev-o/na desno
Second left/right	**Druga na lijevo/na desno**
	drooga na lee-yev-o/na desno
At the crossroads	**Na raskrsnici**
	na rasker-snee-tsee
At the traffic lights	**Na prometna svijetla**
	na prom-etna svee-yet-la
At the roundabout	**Na kružnicu**
	na kroosh-nee-tsoo
At the level crossing	**Na prijelaz preko pruge**
	na pree-yel-az prek-o proog-eh
It's near/far	**Blizu je/daleko je**
	bleez-oo yeh/da-lek-o yeh
One kilometre	**Jedan kilometar**
	yed-an keelo-met-ar
Two kilometres	**Dva kilometra**
	dva keelo-metra
Five minutes . . .	**Pet minuta . . .**
	pet meen-oota . . .
on foot	**pješke**
	p-yesh-keh
by car	**sa kolima**
	sa kol-eema

Take . . .	**Uzmite . . .**
	ooz-mee-teh **. . .**
the bus	**autobus**
	ah-ooto-boos
the train	**vlak**
	vlak
the tram	**tramvaj**
	tramva-ee

[*For public transport, see p. 112*]

The tourist information office

ESSENTIAL INFORMATION

- Most towns and even some coastal villages in Yugoslavia have a tourist information office.
- Look for these words:
  TURISTIČKI INFORMATIVNI CENTAR
  TURISTIČKI URED
  TURISTIČKA AGENCIJA ZA INFORMACIJE
- Sometimes there may be signposts with these abbreviations: **TIC**
- These offices offer you free information in the form of printed leaflets, fold-outs, brochures, lists and plans.
- You may have to pay for some documents but this is not usual.
- For finding a tourist office, see p. 20.

WHAT TO SAY

Please, have you got . . .	**Molim, imate li . . .**
	mol-im *ee*ma-teh lee . . .
a plan of the town?	**plan grada?**
	plan gra-da
a list of hotels?	**katalog hotela?**
	katalog hotel-a
a list of campsites?	**katalog autokampova?**
	katalog *ah*-ooto-kampova
a list of restaurants?	**katalog restorana?**
	katalog restora-na
a list of coach excursions?	**katalog izleta sa autobusom?**
	katalog *eez*-let-a sa *ah*-ootoboos-om
a list of events?	**katalog zabava?**
	katalog zab-ava
a leaflet on the town?	**prospekt grada?**
	prospekt gra-da
a leaflet on the region?	**prospekt pokrajine?**
	prospect pokra-yeeneh
a railway timetable?	**red vožnje?**
	red vosh-nee-yeh
a bus timetable?	**red autobusa?**
	red *ah*-ooto-boosa

In English, please	**Na engleskom jeziku, molim**
	na en-gles-kom yez-eekoo mol-im
How much do I owe you?	**Koliko to košta**
	ko-leeko toh koshta
Can you recommend ...	**Možete li preporučiti ...**
	mosh-et-eh lee preporoo-chit-ee ...
a cheap hotel?	**jeftin hotel?**
	yef-teen hotel
a cheap restaurant?	**jeftin restoran?**
	yef-teen rest-oran?
Can you make a booking for me?	**Možete li rezervirati za mene?**
	mosh-et-eh lee rezair-veer-atee za meh-neh?

LIKELY ANSWERS

You need to understand when the answer is 'No'. You should be able to tell by the assistant's facial expression, tone of voice and gesture; but there are some language clues, such as:

No	**Ne**
	neh
I'm sorry	**Žao mi je**
	sha-o mee yeh
I don't have a list of campsites	**Nemam katalog autokampova**
	neh-mum katalog ah-ooto-kampova
I haven't got any left	**Nemam ni jednog više**
	neh-mum nee yed-nog veesheh
It's free	**To je besplatno**
	toh yeh bes-plat-no

Accommodation

Hotel

ESSENTIAL INFORMATION

- If you want hotel-type accommodation, all the following words in capital letters are worth looking for on name boards:
  HOTEL
  MOTEL
  PANSION (superior boarding house)
- Houses which let rooms privately usually have signs in French, English, German or Italian:
  CHAMBRES/ROOMS/ZIMMER/CAMERE
  Remember that:
- A list of hotels in the town or district can usually be obtained at the local tourist information office [see p. 26].
- Hotels are divided into five classes, pensions into three.
- Not all hotels provide meals, apart from breakfast. (A pension always provides meals). However, for stays of more than three days, hotels and pensions have fixed prices which include accommodation, three meals a day and whatever services are available.
- The cost is displayed in the room itself so you can check it when having a look around before agreeing to stay.
- The displayed cost is for the room itself, per night and not per person.
- Breakfast usually consists of coffee, milk, tea or cocoa with rolls or toast, butter and jam or honey.
- On arrival you will be asked to complete a registration document and the receptionist will want to see your passport and travel documents.
- Tipping is not obligatory but 10% is usual.
- Finding a hotel, see p. 20.

WHAT TO SAY

I have a booking	**Imam rezervirano** *eem-am rezair-veer-ano*
Have you any vacancies, please?	**Imate li praznu sobu, molim?** *eemat-eh lee praz-noo so-boo mol-im*
Can I book a room?	**Mogu li rezervirati sobu?** *mog-oo lee rezair-veer-atee so-boo*
It's for . . .	**To je za . . .** *toh yeh za . . .*
one person	**jednu osobu** *yed-noo os-oboo*
two people	**dvije osobe** *dvee-yeh os-obeh*
[For numbers, see p. 125]	
It's for . . .	**To je za . . .** *toh yeh za . . .*
one night	**jednu noć** *yed-noo noch*
two nights	**dvije noći** *dvee-yeh nochee*
one week	**jednu sedmicu** *yed-noo sedmee-tsoo*
two weeks	**dvije sedmice** *dvee-yeh sedmee-tseh*
I would like . . .	**Želio/željela* bih . . .** *shel-yo/shel-yel-ah beeh . . .*
one room	**jednu sobu** *yed-noo so-boo*
two rooms	**dvije sobe** *dvee-yeh so-beh*
with a single bed	**jednokrevetnu** *yed-nokrev-et-noo*
with two single beds	**dvokrevetnu sa odvojenim krevetima** *dvo-krev-et-noo sa odvo-yen-eem krev-et-eema*
with a double bed	**dvokrevetnu** *dvo-krev-et-noo*
with a toilet	**sa toaletom** *sa twa-leh-tom*

*Men use the first alternative, women the second

I would like . . .(a room)	**Želio/željela* bih. . .(sobu)**
	shel-yo/shel-yel-ah beeh. . .(so-boo)
with a bathroom	**sa kupatilom**
	sa koo-pat-eelom
with a shower	**sa tušom**
	sa too-shom
with a cot	**sa dječjim krevetom**
	sa dee-yech-eem krev-et-om
with a balcony	**sa balkonom**
	sa balkon-om
I would like . . .	**Želio/željela* bih . . .**
	shel-yo/shel-yel-ah beeh . . .
full board	**sa punim pansionom**
	sa poon-eem pansee-onom
bed and breakfast	**sobu i doručak**
	so-boo ee doroo-chak
Do you serve meals?	**Servirate li jela?**
	sairv-eerat-eh lee yel-ah
At what time is . . .	**U koliko sati je . . .**
	oo kol-eeko sa-tee yeh . . .
breakfast?	**doručak**
	doroo-chak
lunch?	**ručak?**
	roochak
dinner?	**večera?**
	vech-era
How much is it?	**Koliko je to?**
	kol-eeko yeh toh
Can I look at the room?	**Mogu li da vidim sobu?**
	mog-oo lee da vee-deem so-boo
I'd prefer a room . . .	**Više volim sobu . . .**
	vee-sheh vol-im so-boo . . .
at the front/at the back	**sa pogledom na ulicu/dvorište**
	sa pog-led-om na ool-itsoo dvoreesh-teh
OK, I'll take it	**Dobro je, uzeti ću je**
	dobro yeh ooz-et-ee choo yeh
No thanks, I won't take it	**Ne hvala, neću je uzeti**
	neh fa-la neh-choo yeh ooz-etee
The key to number (10), please	**Ključ za sobu broj (deset), molim**
	klee-yooch za so-boo broy (deh-set) mol-im

*Men use the first alternative, women the second

Please, may I have ...	**Molim, mogu li dobiti ...** m*o*l-im mog*oo* lee d*o*b-eetee ...
a coat hanger?	**vješalicu?** vee-yesha-leetsoo
a towel?	**ručnik?** r*oo*ch-nik
a glass?	**čašu?** ch*a*sh-oo
some soap?	**sapun?** s*a*p-oon
an ashtray?	**pepeljaru?** p*e*p-el-yar-oo
another pillow?	**još jedan jastuk?** yosh yed-an y*a*s-took
another blanket?	**još jedan pokrivač?** yosh yed-an p*o*k-reevach
Come in!	**Uđite!** *oo*-jee-teh
One moment, please!	**Načas, molim!** n*a*-chas m*o*l-im
Please can you ...	**Molim, možete li ...** m*o*l-im m*o*sh-et-eh lee ...
do this laundry/dry cleaning?	**oprati/očistiti kemijski?** *o*pra-tee/ocheest-ee-tee kem-ee-skee
call me at ...?	**me zvati u ...?** meh zvah-tee oo ...
help me with my luggage?	**mi pomoći sa mojom prtljagon?** mee p*o*m-ochee sa m*o*yom pertl-y*a*-gom
call me a taxi for ...?	**mi zvati taksi za ...?** mee zva-tee t*a*xi za ...

[For times, see p. 128]

The bill, please	**Račun, molim** r*a*ch-oon m*o*l-im
Is service included?	**Je li servis uračunat?** yeh lee s*a*irvis oor*a*ch-oonat
I think this is wrong	**Mislim da ovo nije točno** m*ee*slim da *o*-vo nee-yeh t*o*ch-no
May I have a receipt?	**Želio/željela* bih priznanicu** shel-yo/shel-yeh-ah beeh pr*ee*znan-eetsoo

*Men use the first alternative, women the second

At breakfast

Some more . . . please	**Malo više . . . molim**
	ma-lo veesh-eh . . . mol-im
coffee	**kave**
	ka-veh
tea	**čaja**
	cha-ya
bread	**kruha**
	kroo-ha
butter	**maslaca**
	mas-la-tsa
· marmalade	**marmelade**
	marmela-deh
jam	**djem**
	jam
May I have a soft boiled egg?	**Želio/željela* bih meko kuhano jaje?**
	shel-yo/shel-yel-ah beeh mek-o
	koo-ha-no ya-yeh

LIKELY REACTIONS

Have you an identity document, please?	**Imate li ličnu legitimaciju, molim?**
	eemat-eh lee leech-noo
	leg-eetee-matsee mol-im
What's your name [see p. 16]	**Kako se zovete?**
	ka-ko seh zov-et-eh
Sorry, we're full	**Žao mi je ali smo puni**
	sha-o mee yeh ah-lee smo poon-ee
I haven't any rooms left	**Nemam niti jednu sobu praznu**
	neh-mum neetee yed-noo so-boo
	praz-noo
Do you want to have a look?	**Hoćete li da vidite?**
	hoch-et-eh lee da veed-eet-eh
How many people is it for?	**Za koliko osoba?**
	za kol-eeko os-oba
From (seven o'clock) onwards	**Od (sedam sati) unaprijed**
	od (seh-dam sat-ee) oona-pree-yed
From (midday) onwards	**Od (podne) unaprijed**
[For times, see p. 128]	od (podneh) oona-pree-yed
It's . . . dinars	**To je . . . dinara**
[For numbers, see p. 125]	toh yeh . . . deena-ra

*Men use the first alternative, women the second

Camping and youth hostelling

ESSENTIAL INFORMATION
Camping

- Look for the words: **KAMPING** or **AUTO-CAMP** or this sign.

- Be prepared for the following charges
  per person
  for the car (if applicable)
  for the tent or caravan plot
  for electricity
  for hot showers
- You must provide proof of identity, such as your passport.
- All campsites are state owned and state controlled.
- If you wish to camp off-site, you must obtain a permit from the local tourist office or the municipality.
- On some sites, accommodation is also available in chalets.

Youth hostels

- Look for the word: **OMLADINSKI DOM**
- You must have a YHA card.
- Accommodation is usually provided in small dormitories and you should take your own sleeping bag lining with you.
- Food and cooking facilities vary from place to place and you may also have to help with the domestic chores.
- Accommodation is also available in the student hotels to be found in larger towns which are run by **FERIJALNI SAVEZ** (Yugoslav Youth School Organization).
- **NAROMTRAVEL** which specializes in travel and holidays for young people and students in Yugoslavia also runs its own international youth centres in Dubrovnik, Rovinj and Bečići (near Budva).
- Finding a campsite and a youth hostel, see p. 20
- Replacing equipment, see p. 54.

WHAT TO SAY

I have a booking	**Imam rezervirano**
	eem-am rezair-veer-ano
Have you any vacancies?	**Imate li mjesta?**
	eemat-eh lee m-yesta
It's for . . .	**To je za . . .**
	toh yeh za . . .
one adult	**jednu osoby**
	yed-noo os-oboo
two adults	**dvije osobu**
	dvee-yeh os-obeh
and one child	**i jedno dijete**
	ee yedno dee-yet-eh
and two children	**i dvoje djece**
	ee dvo-yeh dee-yetseh
It's for . . .	**To je za . . .**
	toh yeh za . . .
one night	**jednu noć**
	yed-noo noch
two nights	**dvije noći**
	dvee-yeh nochee
one week	**jednu sedmicu**
	yed-noo sed-mee-tsoo
two weeks	**dvije sedmice**
	dvee-yeh sed-mee-tseh
How much is it . . .	**Koliko je . . .**
	kol-eeko yeh . . .
for the tent?	**za šator?**
	za sha-tor
for the caravan (trailer)?	**za karavanu**
	za karavanoo
for the car?	**za kola?**
	za kola
for the electricity?	**za struju?**
	za stroo-yoo
per person?	**po osobi?**
	po os-obee
per day/night?	**na dan/noć?**
	na dun/noch
May I look round?	**Mogu li pogledati okolo?**
	mog-oo lee pogleh-da-tee okolo
Do you close at night?	**Kada zatvarate noću?**
	ka-da zatvarat-eh nochoo

Do you provide anything . . .   **Mogu li nabaviti nešto . . .**
m*o*g-oo lee n*a*-bav-eetee n*e*sh-to . . .

to eat?   **za jesti?**
za y*e*s-tee

to drink?   **za piti?**
za p*ee*tee

Do you have . . .   **Imate li . . .**
*ee*mat-eh lee . . .

a bar?   **bar?**
bar

hot showers?   **vrući tuš?**
vr*oo*-chee toosh

a kitchen?   **kuhinju?**
k*oo*-heen-yoo

a laundry?   **praonicu?**
pra-*o*nee-tsoo

a restaurant?   **restoran?**
rest-oran

a shop?   **dućan?**
d*oo*ch-an

a swimming pool?   **bazen?**
b*a*z-en

a takeaway?   **snak-bar?**
snack bar

[For food shopping, see p. 61, and for eating and drinking out, see p. 80]

Where are . . .   **Gdje su . . .**
gd-y*e*h soo . . .

the dustbins?   **kante za smeće?**
k*a*nteh za sm*e*h-cheh

the showers?   **tuševi?**
t*oo*shev-ee

the toilets?   **toalete?**
twa-l*e*h-teh

At what time must one . . .   **U koliko sati se mora . . .**
oo k*o*l-eeko s*a*-tee seh m*o*ra . . .

go to bed?   **ići spavati?**
*ee*chee sp*a*va-tee

get-up?   **ustati?**
*oo*sta-tee

Is there . . .   **Ima li tu . . .**
                                  *ee*ma lee too **. . .**

  a broom?   **metla?**
                                  m*e*tla

  a corkscrew?   **vadičep?**
                                  v*a*-deechep

  a drying-up cloth?   **kanavac za sušenje?**
                                  kan*a*-vats za s*oo*sh-en-yeh

  a fork?   **vilica?**
                                  v*ee*l-eetsa

  a fridge?   **frižider?**
                                  frig*i*d-air

  a frying pan?   **tavica?**
                                  t*a*v-eetsa

  an iron?   **pegla?**
                                  p*e*gla

  a knife?   **nož?**
                                  nosh

  a plate?   **tanjur?**
                                  t*a*n-yoor

  a saucepan?   **lonac?**
                                  l*o*n-ats

  a teaspoon?   **mala žlica?**
                                  m*a*-la shl*ee*-tsa

  a tin opener?   **otvarač za konzervu?**
                                  otvar-ach za konz*ai*r-voo

  any washing powder?   **prašak za pranje?**
                                  prash-ak za pr*a*n-yeh

  any washing-up liquid?   **tekućina za pranje?**
                                  tekooch-*ee*na za pr*a*n-yeh

The bill, please   **Račun, molim**
                                  r*a*ch-oon m*o*l-im

Problems

The toilet   **Toaleta**
                                  tw*a*-leh-ta

The shower   **Tuš**
                                  t*oo*sh

The tap   **Slavina**
                                  sl*a*v-eena

The electric point   **Utikač**
                                  *oo*teek-ach

The light	**Svijetlo**
	svee-*yetlo*
. . . is not working	**. . . ne radi**
	neh *ra*-dee
My camping gas has run out	**Nestalo mi je plina**
	neh-stalo mee yeh *plee*-na

LIKELY REACTIONS

Have you an identity document?	**Imate li legitimaciju?**
	*ee*mat-eh lee leg-eetee-*ma*tsee-yoo
Your membership card, please	**Vašu člansku kartu, molim**
	vashoo chlan-skoo kartoo mol-im
What's your name, please? [see p. 16]	**Vaše ime molim?**
	vasheh *ee*meh mol-im
Sorry, we're full.	**Žao mi je ali smo puni**
	sha-o mee yeh *ah*-lee smo poonee
How many people is it for?	**Za koliko osoba?**
	za kol-eeko os-oba
How many nights is it for?	**Za koliko noći?**
	za kol-eeko nochee
It's . . . dinars	**To je . . . dinara**
	toh yeh . . . deena-ra
per day/per night [For numbers, see p. 125]	**na dan/na noć**
	na dun/na noch

Rented accommodation: problem solving

ESSENTIAL INFORMATION

- If you're looking for accommodation to rent, watch for the following signs:
  IZNAJMIVA SE (to let)
  IZNAJMLJUJE SE (to let)
  APARTMANI (apartments)
  SOBE (rooms)
  VILE (villas)
- For arranging details of your let, see 'Hotel', p. 28
- Key words you will meet if renting on the spot:
  depozit (deposit)
  de*pozit*
  ključ (key)
  klee-*yooch*
- Having arranged your own accommodation and arrived with the key, check the obvious basics that you take for granted at home.
  Electricity Voltage? Razors and small appliances brought from home may need adjusting. You may need an adaptor. All light bulbs in Yugoslavia are of the screw-in type, and all plugs have round pins.
  Gas Town gas or bottled gas? Butane gas must be kept indoors, propane gas must be kept outdoors.
  Cooker Don't be surprised to find:
  – the grill inside the oven, or no grill at all.
  – a lid covering the rings which lifts up to form a 'splash-back'
  – a mixture of two gas rings and two electric rings.
  Toilet Mains drainage or septic tank? *Don't* flush disposable nappies or anything else down the toilet, as drainage pipes are very narrow and easily blocked.
  Water Find the stopcock. Check taps and plugs – they may not operate in the way you are used to. Check how to turn on (or light) the hot water.
  Windows Check the method of opening and closing windows and shutters.
  Insects Is an insecticide spray provided? If not, get one locally.
  Equipment For buying or replacing equipment, see p. 54.
- You will probably have an official agent, but be clear in your own mind who to contact in an emergency, even if it is only a neighbour in the first instance.

WHAT TO SAY

My name is . . .	**Moje ime je . . .**
	moyeh *ee*meh yeh . . .
I'm staying at . . .	**Odsjeo/odsjela* sam u . . .**
	od-yeh-o/ods-yel-ah sum oo
They've cut off . . .	**Prekinuli su . . .**
	prek-*ee*noo-lee soo . . .
the electricity	**struju**
	str*oo*-yoo
the gas	**plin**
	pl*ee*n
the water	**vodu**
	vod-oo
Is there . . . in the area?	**Imali ovdje blizu . . .**
	*ee*ma lee ovd-yeh blee-zoo . . .
an electrician	**električar?**
	*e*l-ektree-char?
a plumber	**vodoinstalater?**
	vod-o-insta-la-ter?
a gas fitter	**plinar?**
	pl*ee*nar
Where is . . .	**Gdje je . . .**
	gd-yeh yeh . . .
the fuse box?	**električni osigurač?**
	*e*l-ektreechnee oseeg*oo*-rach?
the stopcock?	**ventil?**
	ven-teel?
the boiler?	**bojler?**
	b*o*iler?
the water heater?	**grijač za vodu?**
	gree-yach za vod-oo?
Is there . . .	**Ima li . . .**
	*ee*ma lee . . .
town gas?/bottled gas?	**gradski plin?/plin u bocama?**
	grat-skee pl*ee*n/pl*ee*n oo botsama
mains drainage?	**kanalizacija?**
	kanalee*za*-tsee-ya
a septic tank?	**septična jama?**
	sept eech-na ya-ma
central heating?	**centralno grijanje?**
	tsentral-no gree-yan-yeh

*Men use the first alternative, women the second

The cooker	**Peć za kuhanje**
	pech za koo-han-yeh
The hairdryer	**Fen za kosu**
	fen za kos-oo
The heating	**Grijanje**
	gree-yan-yeh
The iron	**Pegla**
	pegla
The pilot light	**Kontrolno svijetlo**
	kontrol-no svee-yetlo
The refrigerator	**Frižider**
	frigid-air
The telephone	**Telefon**
	telephon
The toilet	**Toaleta**
	twa-leh-ta
The washing machine	**Stroj za pranje rublja**
	stroy za pran-yeh roobl-ya
The water heater	**Bojler**
	boiler
... is not working	**... ne radi**
	... neh ra-dee
Where can I get ...	**Gdje mogu dobiti ...**
	gd-yeh mog-oo dob-eetee ...
an adaptor for this?	**adapter za ovo?**
	adap-ter za ov-o
a bottle of butane gas?	**bocu plina butana?**
	botsoo pleena boot-ana
a bottle of propane gas?	**bocu plina propana?**
	botsoo pleena prop-an-ah
a fuse?	**električni osigurač?**
	el-ektreechnee oseegoo-rach
an insecticide spray?	**nešto za tamanjenje kukaca?**
	neshto za taman-yen-yeh kook-atsa
a light bulb?	**električnu žarulju?**
	el-ektreechnoo sharool-yoo
The drains are blocked	**Začepio se kanal**
	za-chep-ee-o seh kanal
The sink is blocked	**Začepio se sudoper**
	za-chep-ee-o seh sood-oper
The toilet is blocked	**Začepila se toaleta**
	za-che-pee-la seh twa-leh-ta
The gas is leaking	**Plin propušta**
	pleen prop-oosh-ta

Can you mend it straightaway?	**Možete li ga propraviti odmah?** mosh-et-eh lee ga poprav-eetee odmuh
When can you mend it?	**Kada ga možete popraviti?** ka-dah ga mosh-et-eh poprav-eetee
How much do I owe you?	**Koliko vam dugujem?** kol-eeko vum doog-oo-yem
When is the rubbish collected?	**Kada se kupi smeće?** ka-da seh koopee smeh-cheh

LIKELY REACTIONS

What's your name?	**Vaše ime?** vasheh eemeh
What's your address?	**Koja je vaša adresa?** koya yeh vasha adresa
There's a shop . . .	**Ima dućan** eema doo-chan
in town	**u gradu** oo gra-doo
in the village	**na selu** na seh-loo
I can't come . . .	**Ne mogu doći . . .** neh mog-oo dochee . . .
today	**danas** dan-us
this week	**ove sedmice** ov-eh sedmee-tseh
until Monday	**do ponedjelka** doh poned-yelka
I can come . . .	**Mogu doći . . .** mog-oo dochee . . .
on Tuesday	**u utorak** oo ootorak
when you want	**kad hoćete** kad hoch-et-eh
Every day	**Svaki dan** sva-kee dun
Every other day	**Svaki drugi dan** sva-kee droog-ee dun
On Wednesday	**U srijedu** oo sree-yeh-doo

[For days of the week, see p. 130]

General shopping

The chemist's

ESSENTIAL INFORMATION

- Look for the words **APOTEKA** or **LJEKARNA**, a large cross or this sign:
- Medicines can also be bought at supermarkets or department stores.
- Try the chemist *before* going to a doctor: they are usually qualified to treat minor injuries.
- Chemists are normally open between 8.00 a.m. and 9.00 p.m. However, some 'duty' chemists are open twenty-four hours, look for **DEŽURNA APOTEKA** on the shop door or in the local newspaper.
- Some toiletries can also be bought at a **PARFUMERIJA** but they will be more expensive.
- Finding a chemist, see p. 20.

WHAT TO SAY

I'd like . . .	**Želio/željela* bih . . .**
	shel-yo shel-yel-ah beeh . . .
some Alka Seltzer	**Alku Seltzer**
	alkoo seltzer
some antiseptic	**antiseptičnu mast**
	anti-septeech-noo must
some aspirin	**aspirinu**
	aspee-ree-noo
some bandage	**zavoj**
	tza-voy
some cotton wool	**vatu**
	va-too
some eye drops	**kapi za oči**
	kap-ee za ochee
some foot powder	**puder**
	pooder

*Men use the first alternative, women the second

some gauze dressing	**gazu**
	ga-zoo
some inhalant	**nešto za udisanje**
	neshto za oodee-san-yeh
some insect repellent	**sredstvo protiv insekata**
	sret-stvo prot-eev insek-ata
some lip salve	**pomadu za usne**
	poma-doo za oosneh
some nose drops	**kapi za nos**
	kap-ee za nos
some sticking plaster	**flaster**
	fluster
some throat pastilles	**tablete za grlo**
	tablet-eh za gher-lo
some Vaseline	**vazelin**
	vazel-in
I'd like something for . . .	**Želio/željela* bih nešto za . . .**
	shel-yo/shel-yel-ah beeh
	neshtoo za . . .
bites	**ubode**
	oobod-eh
burns	**opekotine**
	opek-ot-eeneh
chilblains	**ozebline**
	ozeb-leeneh
a cold	**nahladu**
	na-hladoo
constipation	**tvrdu stolicu**
	tver-doo stol-eetsoo
a cough	**kašalj**
	kash-eye
diarrhoea	**proljev**
	prol-yev
earache	**bol uha**
	bohl ooha
flu	**gripu**
	gree-poo
scalds	**oparenje**
	oparen-yeh
sore gums	**upalu desni**
	oop-aloo deh-snee

*Men use the first alternative, women the second

I'd like something for . . .	**Želio/željela* bih nešto za . . .**
	shel-yo/shel-yel-ah beeh
	neshtoo za . . .
sprains	**iščašenje**
	ees-chash-en-yeh
stings	**ubode**
	oobod-eh
sunburn	**opeklinu od sunca**
	opek-lee-noo od soon-tsa
travel sickness	**protiv mučnine**
	prot-eev mooch-neen-eh
I need . . .	**Treba/trebaju* mi . . .**
	treb-a/treba-yoo mee . . .
some baby food	**diječija hrana**
	dee-yech-eeya he-rana
some contraceptives	**kontraceptivno sredstvo**
	kontra-tsep-teev-no sret-stvo
some deodorant	**deodorant**
	deodorant
some disposable nappies	**papirne pelene**
	pap-eer-neh pel-en-eh
some handcream	**krema za ruke**
	krem-a za roo-keh
some lipstick	**ruž za usne**
	roosh za oosneh
some make-up remover	**nešto za čišćenje lica**
	neshto za chee-shen-yeh leetsa
some paper tissues	**papirne maramice**
	pap-eer-neh ma-ram-eetseh
some razor blades	**žilete**
	sheel-et-eh
some safety pins	**pribadača**
	preebada-cha
some sanitary towels	**mjesečne uloške**
	m-yesech-neh oolosh-keh
some shaving cream	**krema za brijanje**
	krem-a za bree-yan-yeh
some soap	**sapun**
	sap-oon
some suntan lotion/oil	**losion/ulje za sunčanje**
	lotion/ool-yeh za soon-chan-yeh

*For singular objects use the first alternative,
  for plural objects use the second

some talcum powder	**talk**
	talc
some Tampax	**Tampax**
	tampax
some (soft) toilet paper	**mekani toaletni papir**
	mek-anee twa-let-nee pap-eer
some toothpaste	**pasta za zube**
	pasta za zoobeh

[For other essential expressions, see 'Shop talk' p. 56]

Holiday items

ESSENTIAL INFORMATION

- Places to shop at and signs to look for:
  PAPIRNICA (stationery)
  KNJIŽARA (bookshop)
  FOTO STUDIO (films)
  and main department stores like: **ROBNA KUĆA**
- If you wish to buy local crafts look for the following sign
  NARODNA RADINOST. These shops, to be found in larger
  towns and tourist resorts, specialize in hand-made embroidery,
  filigree jewellery and ceramics.

WHAT TO SAY

Where can I buy . . . ?	**Gdje mogu kupiti . . . ?** gd-yeh mog-oo koop-eet-ee . . .
I'd like . . .	**Želio/željela* bih . . .** shel-yo/shel-yel-ah beeh . . .
a bag	**torbu** torboo
a beach ball	**loptu za plažu** lop-too za pla-shoo
a bucket	**kantu** kan-to
an English newspaper	**engleske novine** en-gleskeh nov-eeneh
some envelopes	**koverta** kovair-ta
a guide book	**vodiča** vod-eecha
a map (of the area)	**plan okolice** plan ok-ol-eetseh
some postcards	**dopisnica** doh-pees-neetsa
a spade	**lopatu** lop-atoo
a straw hat	**slamnat šešir** slam-nat shesheer

*Men use the first alternative, women the second

a suitcase	**kofer**
	kof-fair
some sunglasses	**naočale za sunce**
	na-och-al-eh za soon-tseh
a sunshade	**suncobran**
	soon-tsobran
an umbrella	**kišobran**
	keesh-obran
some writing paper	**papira za pisanje**
	papeera za pee-san-yeh
I'd like . . .	**Želio/željela* bih . . .**
	shel-yo/shel-yel-ah beeh . . .
[show the camera]	
a colour film	**film u boji**
	film oo boyee
a black and white film	**film crno bijeli**
	film tser-no beeyeh-lee
for prints	**za kopije**
	za kop-ee-yeh
for slides	**za dijapozitiv**
	za deeya-pozitiv
12 (24/36) exposures	**dvanaest (dvadesetčetiri/**
	trideset šest) snimaka
	dva-naest (dva-deh-set chet-eeree/
	tree-deh-set-shehst) sneem-akah
a standard film	**standard film**
	standard film
a super 8 film	**super osam**
	soopair o-sam
some flash bulbs	**fleš lampe**
	flash lam-peh
This camera is broken	**Ovaj foto-aparat je pokvaren**
	ov-eye foto-aparat yeh pok-va-ren
The film is stuck	**Film se zaglavio**
	film seh zaglav-ee-o
Please can you . . .	**Molim, možete li . . .**
	mol-im mosh-et-eh lee . . .
develop this?	**razviti ovo?**
	raz-vee-tee ov-o
load the camera for me?	**staviti film u foto-aparat?**
	stav-eetee film oo foto-aparat

[For other essential expressions, see 'Shop talk', p. 56].

*Men use the first alternative, women the second

The tobacconist's

ESSENTIAL INFORMATION

- A tobacconist's is called **TRAFIKA**. Look also for **DUHAN** – tobacco.
- To ask if there is one near by, see p. 20.
- Nearly all tobacconists sell postage stamps (see p. 100)
- A tobacconist's is sometimes part of a stationer's or newsagents

WHAT TO SAY

A packet of cigarettes . . .	**Kutiju cigareta . . .**
	kootee-yoo tseega-reh-ta . . .
with filters	**sa filterom**
	sa feel-tairom
without filters	**bez filtera**
	bez feel-taira
king size	**duge**
	doog-eh
menthol	**mentol**
	mentol
Those up there . . .	**One tamo gore . . .**
	on-eh ta-mo goreh . . .
on the right	**na desno**
	na des-no
on the left	**na lijevo**
	na lee-yeh-vo
These [point]	**Ove**
	ov-eh
Cigarettes, please	**Cigarete, molim**
	tseega-reh-teh mol-im
100, 200, 300	**Sto, dvjesta, trista**
	sto, dvee-yeh-sta, tree-sta
Two packets	**Dvije kutije**
	dvee-yeh kootee-yeh

Do you have . . .

Imate li . . .
*ee*mat-eh lee . . .

English cigarettes?

engleskih cigareta?
en-gles-keeh tseega-re*h*-ta

American cigarettes?

amerikanskih cigareta?
ame*ri*kan-skeeh tseega-re*h*-tah

English pipe tobacco?

engleskog duhana za lulu?
en-gleskog doo-ha-na za l*oo*loo

American pipe tobacco?

amerikanskog duhana za lulu?
ame*ri*can-skog d*oo*-ha-na za l*oo*loo

rolling tobacco?

duhana za praviti cigarete?
d*oo*-ha-na za pr*a*-veetee
tseega-re*h*-teh

A packet of pipe tobacco

Paket duhana za lulu
packet d*oo*-ha-na za l*oo*loo

That one up there . . .

Taj, tamo gore . . .
t*a*-ee t*a*-mo gor*eh* . . .

on the right

na desno
na d*es*-no

on the left

na lijevo
na lee-y*eh*-vo

This one [*point*]

Ovaj
ov-aee

A cigar, please

Cigar, molim
ts*ee*-gar m*o*l-im

This one [*point*]

Ovaj
ov-aee

Some cigars, please

Cigara, molim
ts*ee*-ga-ra m*o*l-im

Those [*point*]

Te
teh

A box of matches

Kutiju šibica
k*oo*tee-yoo sh*ee*-bee-tsa

A packet of pipe cleaners

Paket čistača za lulu
packet ch*ee*st-acha za l*oo*loo

A packet of flints
   [*show lighter*]

Paket kremenova
packet krem-en-ova

Lighter fuel

Benzin za upaljač
ben-zeen za oop*a*l-yach

Lighter gas, please

plin za upaljač, molim
pleen za oop*a*l-yach m*o*l-im

[*For other essential expressions, see 'Shop talk' p. 56*]

Buying clothes

ESSENTIAL INFORMATION

- Look for:
  ŽENSKA KONFEKCIJA (women's clothes)
  MUŠKA KONFEKCIJA (men's clothes)
  OBUĆA (shoe shop)
- Don't buy without being measured first or without trying things on.
- Don't rely on conversion charts of clothing sizes (see p. 141). If you are buying for someone else, take their measurements with you.

WHAT TO SAY

I'd like . . .	**Želio/željela* bih . . .**
	shel-yo/shel-yel-ah beeh **. . .**
an anorak	**vindjaku**
	wind-yackoo
a belt	**kaiš**
	ka-ish
a bikini	**bikini**
	bikini
a bra	**grudnjak**
	groodn-yak
a cap (swimming)	**kapu (za plivanje)**
	kap-oo (za pleevan-yeh)
a cap (skiiing)	**kapu (za skijanje)**
	kap-oo (za ski-yan-yeh)
a cardigan	**kardigan**
	cardigan
a coat	**kaput**
	kap-ot
a dress	**haljinu**
	hal-yee-noo
a hat	**šešir**
	shesheer
a jacket	**žaket**
	jacket

*Men use the first alternative, women the second

a jumper	**sviter**
	sveeter
a nightdress	**spavaćicu**
	spavach-eetsoo
a pullover	**pulover**
	pullover
a raincoat	**kišni kaput**
	keesh-nee kap-oot
a shirt	**košulju**
	kosh-ool-yoo
a skirt	**suknju**
	sook-nee-yoo
a suit	**odijelo**
	odee-yel-o
a swimsuit	**kupaći kostim**
	koopachee costume
a tee-shirt	**majicu**
	ma-yeetsoo
I'd like . . .	**Želio/željela* bih . . .**
	shel-yo/shel-yel-ah beeh . . .
a pair of pyjamas	**pidžamu**
	peejamoo
a pair of shorts	**šorc**
	shorts
I'd like a pair of . . .	**Želio/željela* bih par . . .**
	shel-yo/shel-yel-ah beeh par . . .
briefs (women)	**gaćica**
	gach-eetsa
gloves	**rukavica**
	rookav-itsa
jeans	**farmerka**
	farmer-ka
socks	**sokne**
	sok-neh
stockings	**čarapa**
	cha-rapa
tights	**hulahopke**
	hoola-hopkeh
trousers	**pantalona**
	pantalona
underpants (men)	**muškíh gaća**
	moosh-keeh gacha

*Men use the first alternative, women the second

I'd like a pair of . . .	Želio/željela* bih par . . .
	shel-yo/shel-yel-ah beeh par . . .
shoes	**cipela**
	tsee-pela
canvas shoes	**patika**
	pat-eeka
sandals	**sandala**
	sandala
beach shoes	**cipela za plažu**
	tsee-pela za plashoo
smart shoes	**elegantnih cipela**
	elegant-neeh tsee-pela
boots	**čizama**
	cheezama
moccasins	**mokasinka**
	mokass-inka
My size is . . .	**Moja mjera je . . .**
[For numbers, see p. 125]	moya mee-yaira yeh . . .
Can you measure me, please?	**Možete li uzeti moje mjere, molim?**
	mosh-et-eh lee oozet-ee moyeh mee-yaireh mo-lim
Can I try it on?	**Mogu li da probam?**
	mog-oo lee da pro-bam
It's for a present	**Ovo je za dar**
	ov-o yeh za dah
These are the measurements	**Ovo su mjere**
[show written]	ov-o soo mee-yaireh
bust	**poprsje**
	popers-yeh
chest	**prsa**
	persa
collar	**ovratnik**
	ovrat-neek
hips	**bokovi**
	bockovee
leg	**noga**
	noga
waist	**pas**
	paas

*Men use the first alternative, women the second

Have you got something . . .	Imate li nešto . . .
	eemat-eh lee neshto . . .
in black?	u crno?
	oo tserno
in white?	u bijelo?
	oo bee-yel-o
in grey?	u sivo?
	oo seevo
in blue?	u plavo?
	oo pla-vo
in brown?	u smedje?
	oo smeh-jeh
in pink?	u roza?
	oo rodza
in green?	u zeleno?
	oo zeleh-no
in red?	u crveno?
	oo tser-ven-o
in yellow?	u žuto?
	oo shoo-to
in this colour? [point]	u ovoj boji?
	oo ov-oy boyee
in cotton?	u pamuku?
	oo pam-ookoo
in denim?	u traper-platnu?
	oo tra-per-platnoo
in leather?	u koži?
	oo kosh-ee
in nylon?	u najlonu?
	oo nylonoo
in suede?	u jelenoj koži?
	oo yel-en-oy kosh-ee
in wool?	u vuni?
	oo voonee
in this material? [point]	u ovoj tkanini?
	oo ov-oy t-kan-eenee

[For other essential expressions, see 'Shop talk', p. 56]

*Men use the first alternative, women the second

Replacing equipment

ESSENTIAL INFORMATION

- Look for these shops:
  ŽELJEZARA (hardware)
  ELEKTRIČNI MATERIJAL (electrical goods)
- In a supermarket, look for this display **ŽELJEZNARIJA**
- To ask the way to the shop, see p. 20
- At a campsite try their shop first, if there is one.

WHAT TO SAY

Have you got . . .	Imate li . . . *ee*mat-eh-lee . . .
an adaptor? [*show appliance*]	**adaptor?** ad*a*p-tor
a bottle of butane gas?	**bocu butana plina?** b*o*tsoo b*oo*t-ana pl*ee*na
a bottle of propane gas?	**bocu propana plina?** b*o*tsoo pr*o*p-ana pl*ee*na
a bottle opener?	**vadičep?** vad*ee*-chep
any disinfectant?	**sredstvo za dezinfekciju?** sr*e*t-stvo za dezeen-f*e*k-tsee-yoo
any disposable cups?	**papirne šalice?** p*a*p-eer-neh sh*a*l-eetseh
any disposable plates?	**papirne tanjure?** p*a*p-eer-neh tan-y*oo*-reh
a drying up cloth?	**krpu za sušenje?** k*e*r-poo za s*oo*-shen-yeh
any forks?	**vilica?** v*ee*l-eetsa
a fuse? [*show old one*]	**električni osigurač?** *e*-ektreechnee oseeg*oo*-rach?
an insecticide spray?	**sprej za tamanjenje kukaca?** spray za tam*a*n-yen-yeh k*oo*ka-tsa
a kitchen roll? (paper)	**papira za kuhinju?** pap*ee*-ra za k*oo*-heen-yoo
any knives?	**noža?** n*o*sha

a light bulb	**žarulju?**
[*show old one*]	sh*ar*-ool-yoo
a plastic bucket?	**kantu od plastike?**
	k*an*-too od pl*a*st-ee-keh
a plastic can?	**limenku od plastike?**
	l*ee*men-koo od pl*a*st-ee-keh
a scouring pad?	**žicu za posudje?**
	sh*ee*tsoo za p*os*-oojeh
a spanner?	**ključ za matice?**
	klee-y*oo*ch za mat*ee*-tseh
a sponge?	**spužvu?**
	sp*oo*sh-voo
any string?	**špaga?**
	shp*a*-ga
any tent pegs?	**štipaljke za šator?**
	sht*ee*pal-keh za sh*a*-tor
a tin opener?	**otvarač za konzerve?**
	ot-varach za k*o*nzair-veh
a torch?	**džepnu lampu**
	j*e*pnoo l*a*mpoo
any torch batteries?	**baterije za džepnu lampu?**
	bat*ai*ree-yeh za j*e*pnoo l*a*mpoo
a universal plug (for the sink)?	**univerzalan čep (za pilo)**
	ooniv*ai*r-zalan chep (za p*ee*lo)
a washing line?	**konopac za sušenje rublja?**
	k*o*no-pats za s*oo*shen-yeh r*oo*bl-ya
any washing powder?	**prašak za pranje rublja?**
	pr*a*shak za pr*a*n-yeh r*oo*bl-ya
a washing-up brush?	**četku za pranje?**
	chet-k*oo* za pr*a*n-yeh
any washing-up liquid?	**tekućinu za pranje sudja?**
	tekooch-*ee*noo za pr*a*n-yeh s*oo*d-ya

[*For other essential expressions, see 'Shop talk', p. 56*]

Shop talk

ESSENTIAL INFORMATION

- Know your coins and notes
  coins: see illustration.
  notes: 5, 10, 20, 50, 100, 500, 1000 dinara
- Know how to say the important weights and measures:
  [*For numbers, see p. 125*]

50 grams	**Pedeset grama**
	peh-deh-set gra-ma
100 grams	**Sto grama**
	sto gra-ma
200 grams	**Dvjesta grama**
	dvee-yeh-sta gra-ma
½ kilo	**Pola kila**
	pol-a keela
1 kilo	**Kilo**
	keelo
2 kilos	**Dva kila**
	dva keela
½ litre	**Pola litre**
	pol-a leetreh
1 litre	**Litra**
	leetra
2 litres	**Dvije litre**
	dvee-yeh leetreh

- In small shops don't be surprised if customers, as well as the
  shop assistant, say 'hello' and 'goodbye' to you.

CUSTOMER

Hello	**Dobar dan**
	dob-ar dun
Good morning	**Dobro jutro**
	dob-ro yootro
Good afternoon	**Dobar dan**
	dob-ar dun
Goodbye	**Zbogom**
	zbog-om
I'm just looking	**Samo gledam**
	sa-mo gled-am
Excuse me	**Oprostite**
	oprost-eet-eh
How much is this/that?	**Koliko košta ovo/to?**
	kol-eeko koshta ov-o/toh
What is that?	**Što je to?**
	shto yeh toh
What are those?	**Što su te?**
	shto soo teh
Is there a discount?	**Ima li popusta?**
	eema lee pop-oosta
I'd like that, please	**Želio/željela* bih to molim**
	shel-yo/shel-yel-ah beeh toh mol-im
Not that	**Ne to**
	neh toh
Like that	**Onako**
	on-a-ko
That's enough, thank you	**To je dosta, hvala**
	toh yeh dosta fa-la
More please	**Više, molim**
	veesheh mol-im
Less	**Manje od toga**
	man-yeh od tog-a
That's fine	**To je dobro**
	toh yeh dob-ro
OK	**Dobro je**
	dob-ro yeh
I won't take it, thank you	**Neću to, hvala vam**
	nech-oo toh fa-la vum

*Men use the first alternative, women the second

It's not right	**Nije točno**
	nee-yeh toch-no
Thank you very much	**Velika vam hvala**
	vel-eeka vum fa-la
Have you got something . . .	**Imate li nešto . . .**
	eemat-eh lee neshto . . .
better?	**bolje?**
	bol-yeh
cheaper?	**jevtinije?**
	yeft-een-yeh
different?	**različitije?**
	razleech-eet-yeh
larger?	**veće?**
	veh-cheh
smaller?	**manje?**
	man-yeh
At what time do you . . .	**U koliko sati . . .**
	oo kol-eeko sa-tee . . .
open?	**otvarate?**
	otvara-teh
close?	**zatvarate?**
	zatvara-teh
Can I have a bag, please?	**Mogu li da dobijem kesicu, molim?**
	mog-oo lee da dob-ee-yem
	kes-eetsoo mol-im
Can I have a receipt?	**Mogu li da dobijem priznanicu?**
	mog-oo lee da dob-ee-yem
	preeznan-eetsoo
Do you take . . .	**Primate li . . .**
	preemat-eh lee . . .
English/American money?	**engleski/amerikanski novac?**
	en-gleskee/amerikan-skee nov-ats
travellers' cheques?	**putne čekove?**
	poot-neh check-oveh
credit cards?	**Kreditne karte?**
	cred-eetneh karteh
I'd like . . .	**Želio/željela* bih . . .**
	shel-yo/shel-yel-ah beeh . . .
one like that	**jedan kao taj**
	yed-an kow ta-ee
two like that	**dva kao ti**
	dva kow teeh

*Men use the first alternative, women the second

SHOP ASSISTANT

Can I help you?	**Mogu li vam pomoći?**
	mog-oo lee vum pom-ochee
What would you like?	**Što želite?**
	shto shel-eeteh
Is that all?	**Je li to sve?**
	yeh lee toh sveh
Anything else?	**Nešto drugo?**
	neshto droogo
Would you like it wrapped?	**Želite li da vam zamotam?**
	shel-eeteh lee da vum zamot-an
Sorry, none left	**žao mi je nemamo više**
	sha-o mee yeh nem-amo veesheh
I haven't got any	**Nemam ni jedan**
	nem-am nee yed-an
I haven't got any more	**Nemam više**
	nem-am veesheh
How many do you want?	**Koliko ih želite?**
	kol-eeko shel-eeteh
Is that enough?	**Je li to dosta?**
	yeh lee toh dosta?

Shopping for food

Bread

ESSENTIAL INFORMATION

- Finding a baker's, see p. 20
- Key words to look for:
  PRODAVAONICA KRUHA
  PEKARNA
  TRGOVINA KRUHA
- Mini-markets, supermarkets of any size and general stores nearly always sell bread.
- Opening times: 7.00/7.30 a.m. – 12.00 p.m. and 5.00 p.m. – 8.00 p.m. Saturday: 7.00/7.30 a.m. to 12.00 p.m.
- The most characteristic type of loaves in Croatia are **pogača** which are large, flat and round. However, the words for the various types of bread differ throughout Yugoslavia and you should be prepared to point to what you want.

WHAT TO SAY

Some bread, please	**Kruha, molim** krooha mol-im
One loaf (like that)	**Jednu pogaču (kao tu)** yed-noo pog-achoo (kow too)
A large one	**Veliku** vel-eekoo
A small one	**Malu** mal-oo
One bread roll	**Jednu rusicu** yed-noo roo-see-tsoo
250 grams of . . .	**Dvjesta pedeset grama . . .** dvee-yeh-sta peh-deh-set gra-ma . . .
½ kilo of . . .	**Pola kile . . .** pol-a keeleh . . .
1 kilo of . . .	**Kilo . . .** keelo . . .
bread	**kruha** krooha

1 kilo of . . .	**Kilo . . .**
	keelo . . .
white bread	**bijelog kruha**
	bee-yel-og krooha
wholemeal bread	**crnog kruha**
	tser-nog krooha
bread rolls	**rusica**
	roo-see-tsa
Two loaves	**Dvije pogače**
	dvee-yeh pog-acheħ
Four bread rolls	**Četiri rusice**
	chet-eeree roo-see-tsch

[*For other essential expressions, see 'Shop talk', p. 56*]

Cakes

ESSENTIAL INFORMATION

- Key word to look for:
  SLASTIČARNA (cake shop)
- To find a cake shop, see p. 20.
- KAVANA is a place where cakes can be bought to be eaten on the premises or taken away – alcoholic drinks are also served.
- Ordering a drink, see p. 80.

WHAT TO SAY

The type of cakes you find in the shops varies from region to region but the following are some of the most common.

doboš torta	chocolate layer cake with glazed
doh-bosh torta	sugar topping
hladna krema	custard pie
ladna krem-a	
krafen	doughnut
kraf-en	
krem pita	custard cake
krem peeta	
išler	éclair
eesh-ler	

narcapan nartsapan	marzipan
ita od jabuka eeta od ya-booka	apple strudel
ita od sira eeta od seera	cheese cake
rinces krafne rinces kraf-neh	cream doughnut
rokut rok-oot	mille feuilles
ampita hampeeta	tart with whipped cream and meringue mixture

You usually buy medium-size cakes by number:

One doughnut	**Jedan krafen** yed-an kraf-en
Two doughnuts, please	**Dva krafena, molim** dva kraf-en-a mol-im

You buy small cakes by weight:

200 grams of biscuits	**Dvjesta grama keksa** dvee-yeh-sta gra-ma kex-ah
400 grams of petit fours	**Četrsto grama kolačića** chet-ersto gra-ma kolach-ee-cha

You may want to buy a larger cake by the slice:

One slice of apple cake	**Jedan komad štrudela** yed-an kom-ad shtrood-la
Two slices of almond cake	**Dva komada torte od badema** dva kom-a-da torteh od ba-dem-a

You may also want to say:

A selection, please	**Miješanih, molim** mee-yesh-aneeh mol-im

[For other essential expressions, see 'Shop talk', p. 56]

Ice-cream and sweets

ESSENTIAL INFORMATION

- Key words to look for:
  SLADOLED (ice cream)
  SLASTIČARNA (cake shop)
- Prepacked sweets are available in general stores, supermarket and ice-cream stalls in the streets. There is no Yugoslav equivalent of a sweet shop.

WHAT TO SAY

A . . . ice, please	**Sladoled . . . molim**
	sla-doh-led . . . mol-im
banana	**od banana**
	od banana
chocolate	**od čokolade**
	od chokola-deh
hazelnut	**od lješnjaka**
	od l-yeh-shen-yaka
raspberry	**od malina**
	od ma-leena
strawberry	**od jagoda**
	od ya-goda
vanilla	**od vanilje**
	od vaneel-yeh
A single	**Jedan**
	yed-an
Two singles	**Dva**
	dva
A double	**Jedan dupli**
	yed-an doop-lee
Two doubles	**Dva dupla**
	dva doopla
A cone	**Kornet**
	kor-net

A packet of . . .	**Paket . . .**
	p*a*ck-et
100 grams of . . .	**Sto grama . . .**
	sto gr*a*-ma . . .
200 grams of . . .	**Dvjesta grama . . .**
	dvee-yeh-sta gr*a*-ma . . .
sweets	**slatkiša**
	slat-k*ee*sha
toffees	**štolvera**
	sht*o*l-vera
chocolates	**čokolade**
	chokol*a*-deh
mints	**mentina**
	ment*ee*na
A lollipop	**Lilihipa**
	l*i*lly-heep

[For other essential expressions, see 'Shop talk' p. 56]

In the supermarket

ESSENTIAL INFORMATION

- The place to ask for:
  ROBNA KUĆA (department store**)**
  SUPERMARKET
  MINIMARKET
  ŽIVEŽNE NAMIRNICE (general food store**)**
- Key instructions on signs in the shop:
  ULAZ (entrance)
  ZABRANJEN ULAZ (no entry)
  IZLAZ (exit)
  ZABRANJEN IZLAZ (no exit)
  NEMA IZLAZA (no way out)
  BLAGAJNA (cash desk)
  PONUDE (on offer)
  SAMOPOSLUGA (self-service)
- Most supermarkets are open throughout the day during the week and on Saturday mornings. Some self-service shops also open on Sunday mornings.
- No need to say anything in a supermarket, but ask if you can't see what you want.

WHAT TO SAY

Excuse me, please	**Izvinite, molim Vas**
	eez-veen-eeteh mol-im vus
Where is . . .	**Gdje je . . .**
	gd-yeh yeh . . .
the bread?	**kruh?**
	krooh
the butter?	**maslac?**
	mas-lats
the cheese?	**sir?**
	seer
the chocolate?	**čokolada?**
	chokola-da
the coffee?	**kava?**
	ka-va

the cooking oil?	**ulje za kuhanje?**
	ool-yeh za k*oo*-han-yeh
the frozen food?	**zaledjena hrana?**
	zal*ej*-en-a hr*ah*-na
the fruit?	**voće?**
	*vo*cheh
the fruit juice?	**voćni sok?**
	voch-nee soak
the jam?	**djem?**
	jam
the meat?	**meso?**
	m*eh*-so
the milk?	**mlijeko?**
	mlee-*yek*-o
the mineral water?	**mineralna voda?**.
	m*ee*nairal-na v*od*-a
the pasta?	**pasta?**
	p*a*sta
the salt?	**sol?**
	sol
the sugar?	**šećer?**
	sh*ech*er
the tea?	**čaj?**
	cha-ee
the tinned fish?	**konzervirana riba**
	konz*airv*-eekana r*ee*ba
the tinned fruit?	**konzervirano voće**
	konz*airv*-eekano v*oche*h
the vegetable section?	**povrće?**
	p*ov*-ercheh
the vinegar?	**ocat?**
	ots-at
the wine?	**vino?**
	v*ee*no
the yogurt?	**yogurt?**
	y*o*gourt
Where are . . .	Gdje su . . .
	gd-yeh soo . . .
the biscuits?	**keksi?**
	k*ex*-ee
the crisps?	**krisps?**
	crisps

Where are . . .	**Gdje su . . .**
	gd-yeh soo . . .
the eggs?	**jaja?**
	ya-ya
the seafoods?	**morski školjkari?**
	mors-kee shkol-karee
the snails?	**puži**
	poo-shee
the soft drinks?	**nealkoholna pića?**
	nehalkohol-na peechah
the sweets?	**slatkiši**
	slat-keeshee
the tinned vegetables?	**konzervirano povrće?**
	konzairv-eerano pov-ercheh

[*For other essential expressions, see 'Shop talk', p. 56*]

Picnic food

ESSENTIAL INFORMATION

- Key words to look for:
  DELIKATESNA RADNJA (delicatessen)
  MESARNICA (butcher's)
  ŽIVEŽNE NAMIRNICE (grocer's)
- Weight guide:
  4–6 oz/150 g of prepared salad per two people, if eaten as a starter
  to a substantial meal.
  3–4 oz/100 g of prepared salad per person, if to be eaten as the
  main part of a picnic-style meal.

WHAT TO SAY

One slice of . . .	**Jedan odrezak** . . .
	yed-an od-rez-ak . . .
Two slices of . . .	**Dva odreska**
	dva od-res-ka . . .
roast beef	**govedjeg pečenja**
	gov-ed-yeg pech-en-ya
roast pork	**svinjskog pečenja**
	sveen-skog pech-en-ya
tongue	**jezika**
	yez-eeka
ham	**šunke**
	shoonkeh
paté	**paštete**
	pash-teh-teh
garlic sausage	**kobasica**
	kobas-eetsah
salami	**salame**
	salam-eh
100 grams of . . .	**Sto grama** . . .
	sto gra-ma . . .
150 grams of . . .	**Sto pedeset grama** . . .
	sto peh-deh-set gra-ma . . .
200 grams of . . .	**Dvjesta grama** . . .
	dvee-yeh-sta gra-ma

300 grams of . . .	Trista grama . . .
	tree-sta gra-ma
russian salad	**ruske salate**
	roosk-eh sal-at-eh
tomato salad	**salate of paradajza**
	sal-at-eh od parada-ee za
beetroot salad	**salate od cikle**
	sal-at-eh od tseek-leh
mixed salad	**mješane salate**
	m-yeshan-eh sal-at-eh
carrot salad	**salate od mrkve**
	sal-at-eh od merk-veh
green salad	**salate zelene**
	sal-at-eh zel-en-eh
olives	**maslina**
	musleena
anchovies	**inćuna**
	eenchoona
cheese	**sira**
	seera

You might also like to try some of these:

dalmatinski pršut	ham from Dalmatia
dalmat-eenskee per-shoot	
dimljeni sir	smoked cheese
diml-yen-ee seer	
domaće kobasice	homemade sausages
domacheh kobas-eetseh	
domaći sir	local cheese
domachee seer	
jastog	lobster
yast-og	
kajmak	rich soft cheese made from scalded
ka-eemuk	milk
kamenice	oysters
kamen-eetseh	
kranjske kobasice	sausages from Slovenia
kran-yes-keh kobas-eetseh	
kuhana šunka	cooked ham
koohana shoon-ka	
marinirana riba	marinated fish
marin-eerana reeba	

mliječni sir	milk cheese
mlee-yech-nee seer	
pašteta od džigerice	liver paté
pash-teh-ta od jeeg-eritseh	
pašteta od mesa	meat paté
pash-teh-ta od meh-sa	
paški sir	cheese from Pag island
pash-kee seer	
pečena guska	roast goose
pech-ena gooska	
pečena patka	roast duck
pech-ena patka	
pečeno pile	roast chicken
pech-eno peeleh	
pečena teletina	roast veal
pech-ena teh-leh-teena	
pohano meso	fried meat in breadcrumbs
po-hano meh-soh	
pohano pile	fried chicken in breadcrumbs
po-hano peeleh	
punjena jaja	stuffed eggs
poon-yen-ah ya-ya	
sardine	sardines
sardeeneh	
sir sa vrhnjem	curd cheese with sour cream
seer sa verhen-yem	
sušene haringe	smoked herrings
sooshen-eh har-een-gheh	
trapist	ewe's milk cheese (firm and mild)
trap-eest	
tunjevina	tuna fish
toon-yev-eena	

[*For other essential expressions, see 'Shop talk', p. 56*]

Fruit and vegetables

ESSENTIAL INFORMATION

- Key words to look for:
  VOĆE (fruit)
  VOĆARNA (fruit shop)
  POVRĆE (vegetables)
- If possible, buy fruit and vegetables in the market where they are cheaper and fresher than in the shops. Open air markets are held in most areas.
- It is customary for you to choose your own fruit and vegetables at the market (and in some shops) and for the stallholder to weigh and price them. You must take your own shopping bag: paper and plastic bags are not normally provided.
- Weight guide: 1 kilo of potatoes is sufficient for six people for one meal.

WHAT TO SAY

½ kilo (1 lb) of . . .	**Pola kila . . .**
	pol-ah *keela* . . .
1 kilo of . . .	**Kilo . . .**
	keelo . . .
2 kilos of . . .	**Dva kila . . .**
	dva keela . . .
apples	**jabuka**
	ya-booka
apricots	**marelica**
	mar-el-eetsa
bananas	**banana**
	banana
cherries	**trešanja**
	treshan-ya
figs	**smokve**
	smok-veh
grapes (white/black)	**groždja (bijeloga/crnoga)**
	grosh-ja (bee-yeloga/tsernoga)
oranges	**naranača**
	naran-acha
pears	**kruśaka**
	kroosha-ka

peaches	**breskava**
	bresk-ava
plums	**šljiva**
	shl-*eeva*
strawberries	**jagoda**
	y*a*-goda
A pineapple, please	**Ananas, molim**
	*a*nanas mol-im
A grapefruit	**Grejpfrut**
	gr*a*pefruit
A melon	**Dinju**
	d*ee*n-yoo
A water melon	**Lubenicu**
	l*oo*ben-eetsoo
250 grams of ...	**Dvjesta pedeset grama ...**
	dvee-yeh-sta peh-deh-set gr*a*-ma ...
½ kilo of ...	**Pola kila ...**
	pol-a k*ee*la ...
1 kilo of ...	**Kilo ...**
	k*ee*lo ...
1½ kilos of ...	**Kilo i po ...**
	k*ee*lo ee po ...
2 kilos of ...	**Dva kila ...**
	dv*a*h k*ee*la ...
aubergines	**melancane**
	mel*a*n-tsaneh
beans	**graha**
	gr*a*-ha
carrots	**mrkve**
	merk-veh
courgettes	**tikvice**
	t*ee*k-veetseh
green beans	**mahuna**
	mah*oo*-na
leeks	**poriluka**
	por*ee*l-ook*a*
mushrooms	**gljiva**
	gl*ee*va
onions	**luka**
	l*oo*ka
peas	**graška**
	gr*a*shka
potatoes	**krompira**
	kromp-*ee*ra

2 kilos of . . .	**Dva kila . . .**
	dv*a*h k*ee*la . . .
spinach	**spanaća**
	span*a*cha
tomatoes	**paradajza**
	parad*a*-eez*a*
A bunch of . . .	**Kitu . . .**
	k*ee*too . . .
parsley	**peršuna**
	persh-*oo*na
radishes	**rotkvica**
	r*o*t-kvee-tsa
A head of garlic	**Glava češnjaka**
	gl*a*va cheshn-y*a*-k*a*
A lettuce	**Salata**
	s*a*l-ata
A cauliflower	**Karfiol**
	karf*ee*-ol
A cabbage	**Kupus glavati**
	k*oo*poos gl*a*v-atee
A cucumber	**Krastavac**
	kras-tavats
A turnip	**Repa**
	rep-a
Like that, please	**Tako, molim vas**
	tak-o mol-im vus

Fruit and vegetables which may not be familiar:

blitva	beet leaf: like a large stalky
bl*ee*tva	spinach leaf
nešpola	medlar: small, slightly sour fruit,
nesh-pol-a*h*	orange colour, juicy
šipak	pomegranate
sh*ee*pak	
višnja	morello cherry
v*ee*shneeya	
žučenica	young dandelion leaf, used in
shoochen-eetsa	salads

[*For other essential information, see 'Shop talk' p. 56*]

Meat

ESSENTIAL INFORMATION

- Key words to look for:
  MESARNICA or **MESNICA** (butcher's)
  MESAR (butcher)
- Weight guide: 4-6 ozs/125–200 g of meat per person for one meal.
- The meat is not displayed in the same way as in the UK, nor should you expect to find the same cuts. However, you should tell the butcher whether you intend to boil, to grill or to roast the meat so that he will know what to give you.

WHAT TO SAY

For a joint, choose the type of meat and then say how many people it is for and how you intend to cook it:

Some beef, please	**Komad govedine, molim**
	kom-ad gov-ed-eeneh mol-im
Some lamb	**Komad janjetine**
	kom-ad yan-yet-eeneh
Some mutton	**Komad ovčetine**
	kom-ad ov-chet-eeneh
Some pork	**Komad svinjetine**
	kom-ad sveen-yet-eeneh
Some veal	**Komad teletine**
	kom-ad teh-leh-teeneh
A joint . . .	**Komad . . .**
	kom-ad . . .
for two people	**za dvije osobe**
	za dvee-yeh os-obeh
for four people	**za četiri osobe**
	za chet-eeree os-obeh
for six people	**za šest osoba**
	za shehst os-oba
to boil	**za kuhati**
	za koo-hat-ee
to grill	**za na roštilju**
	za nah rosh-teel-yoo
to roast	**za peći**

For steak, liver or kidneys, do as above

Some steak, please	**Biftek, molim**
	bee*f*tek m*o*l-im
Some liver	**Jetre**
	yet-reh
Some kidneys	**Bubrega**
	boob-reg-ah
Some sausages	**Kobasice**
	kob*a*s-eetseh
for three people	**za tri osobe**
	za tr*ee* os-obeh
for five people	**za pet osoba**
	za pet os-obah

For chops do it this way:

Two veal escalopes, please	**Dvije teleće šnicle, molim**
	dv*ee*-yeh teh-lech-eh shn*ii*ts-leh m*o*l-im
Three pork chops	**Tri svinjska kotleta**
	tr*ee* sveen-ska kot-leh-ta
Four mutton chops	**Četiri ovčja kotleta**
	chet-eeree ov-chee-ya kot-leh-ta
Five lamb chops	**Pet janjećih kotleta**
	peht yan-yech-eeh kot-leh-ta

You may also want:

A chicken	**Pile**
	peeleh
A rabbit	**Kunić**
	koonich
A tongue	**Jezik**
	yez-eek

Other essential expressions [see *also p. 56*]

Please can you . . .	**Molim vas možete li . . .**
	m*o*l-im vus m*o*sh-et-eh lee . . .
mince it?	**faširati?**
	fash-eer-atee
dice it?	**izrezati na kocke?**
	eezrez-atee na kots-keh
trim the fat?	**otkinuti debelo?**
	*o*tkee-noo-tee deb-el-oh

Fish

ESSENTIAL INFORMATION

- The place to ask for: **RIBARNICA** (fishmonger's)
- Markets usually have fish stalls.
- Weight guide: 8 oz/250 g minimum per person for one meal of fish bought on the bone.
  i.e. ½ kilo/500 g   for two people
      1 kilo   for four people
      1½ kilos   for six people
- It is not normal practice in Yugoslavia for the fishmonger to fillet fish, and you may also find that some fishmongers will not clean fish, so check beforehand.

WHAT TO SAY

Purchase large fish and small shellfish by weight:

½ kilo of . . .	**Pola kila . . .**
	pol-a keela . . .
1 kilo of . . .	**Kilo . . .**
	keelo . . .
1½ kilos of . . .	**Kilo i po . . .**
	keelo ee po . . .
bass	**brancina**
	bran-tseena
carp	**šarana**
	shar-ana
squid	**liganja**
	leegan-ya
cod (dried)	**bakalara**
	bakalar-ah
cod (fresh)	**svježog bakalara**
	svye-shog bakalar-ah
eels	**jegulja**
	yeg-ool-ya
grey mullet	**cipola**
	tseep-ola
lobster	**jastoga**
	yas-tog-ah

1½ kilos of . . .	Kilo i po . . .
	keelo ee po . . .
mussels	mušula
	moosh-oola
oysters	kamenica
	kamen-eetsa
prawns	gambora
	gambora
red mullet	barbuna
	barboona
scampi	škampija
	shkam-peea
sole	listova
	leestova
pilchards	sardela
	sard-ela

Some large fish can be purchased by the slice:

One slice of . . .	Komad . . .
	kom-ad . . .
Two slices of . . .	Dva komada . . .
	dva kom-a-da . . .
Six slices of . . .	Šest komada . . .
	shehst kom-a-da . . .
salmon	lososa
	los-os-a
cod	bakalara
	bakalar-a
fresh tuna	tunjevine
	toon-jev-eeneh

For some shellfish and 'frying pan' fish, say the name and then specify the number you want [*For numbers, see p. 125*]

A crab	Rak
	rak mol-im
A lobster	Jastog
	yas£tog
A whiting	Merlan
	mair-lan
An ink fish	Sipa
	seepa

An octopus	**Hobotnica**
	hob-otneetsah
A sole	**List**
	leest
A trout	**Pastrva**
	past-erva
A mackerel	**Lokarda**
	lok-arda
A herring	**Haringa**
	har-eenga
A pike	**Štuka**
	*shtoo*ka
A carp	**Šaran**
	shar-an

Other essential expressions [*see also p. 56*]

Please can you . . .	**Molim vas možete li . . .**
	mol-im vus *mosh*-et-eh lee . . .
take the heads off?	**otkinuti glave?**
	ot-kee-noo-tee gla-veh
clean them?	**očistiti ih?**
	*o*cheest-eetee

Eating and drinking out

Ordering a drink

ESSENTIAL INFORMATION

- The place to ask for: **KAVANA** (see p. 20)
- By law, the price list of drinks must be displayed outside or in the window.
- There is waiter service in all cafés, but you can drink at the bar or counter if you wish (cheaper).
- Always leave a tip of 10%-15% of the bill unless you see **SERVIS UKLJUČEN** (service included) printed on the bill or on a notice.
- Cafés serve non-alcoholic drinks and alcoholic drinks, and are normally open all day. Children may accompany their parents into bars.
- Local mineral water is available.
- The following list of drinks are all local brandies which you may like to try: **kajsjevača** (apricot brandy), **komovica** (brandy made from grape-pressings), **orahovica** (brandy made from grape pressings with green shells of walnuts in it), **rakija** (brandy from fruit pressings), **šljivovica** (plum brandy).

WHAT TO SAY

I'll have . . .	**Htio/htjela* bih . . .**
	ht*ee*-o/ht-y*e*lah beeh **. . .**
a black coffee	**crnu kavu**
	ts*e*r-noo k*a*-voo
a coffee with cream	**kavu sa šlagom**
	k*a*-voo sa shl*ag*-om
a tea	**čaj**
	ch*a*-ee
with milk	**sa mlijekom**
	sa mlee-y*e*k-om
with lemon	**sa limunom**
	sa l*ee*moon-om
a glass of milk	**čašu mlijeka**
	ch*a*sh-oo mlee-y*e*k-a
two glasses of milk	**dvije čaše mlijeka**
	dv*ee*-yeh ch*a*sh-eh mlee-y*e*k-a

*Men use the first alternative, women the second

a hot chocolate	**kakao**
	kak*a*-o
a mineral water	**mineralnu vodu**
	m*ee*nairal-noo v*o*d-oo
a lemonade	**limunadu**
	leemoon*a*-doo
a lemon squash	**sok limuna**
	s*o*ak leem*oo*na
a Coca Cola	**koka-kolu**
	c*o*ca-col*oo*
an orangeade	**oranžadu**
	oranj*a*-doo
an orange juice	**sok od naranče**
	s*o*ak od n*a*ran-cheh
a grape juice	**sok od gr02dja**
	s*o*ak od gr*o*sh-ja
a pineapple juice	**sok od ananasa**
	s*o*ak od *a*nanasa
a small bottle of beer	**malu bocu pive**
	m*a*-loo b*o*tsoo p*ee*veh
a large bottle of beer	**veliku bocu pive**
	v*e*l-eekoo b*o*tsoo p*ee*veh
A glass of . . .	**Čašu . . .**
	ch*a*sh-oo . . .
Two glasses of . . .	**Dvije čaše . . .**
	dv*ee*-yeh ch*a*sh-eh . . .
red wine	**crnog vina**
	ts*e*r-nog v*ee*na
white wine	**bijelog vina**
	bee-y*e*l-og v*ee*na
rosé wine	**ružičastog vina**
	r*oo*sh-chast-og v*ee*na
sparkling wine	**pjenušava vina**
	pee-y*e*n-oosh-ava v*ee*na
champagne	**šampanjca**
	shamp*a*ntsa
A whisky . . .	**Viski . . .**
	v*i*skey . . .
with ice	**sa ledom**
	sa l*e*d-om
with water	**sa vodom**
	sa v*o*d-om
with soda	**sa sodom**
	sa s*o*d-om

Ordering a snack

ESSENTIAL INFORMATION

- Look for a café or bar with these signs:
  BAR
  BIFE (snack bar)
  GRILL
- Look for the names of snacks (listed below) on signs in the window.
- In some regions mobile vans sell hot snacks.
- For cakes, see p. 62.
- For ice-cream, see p. 64.
- For picnic-type snacks, see p. 69.

WHAT TO SAY

I'll have . . . please	**Molim vas htio/htjela* bih . . .** mol-im vus htee-o/ht-yelah beeh **. . .**
a cheese sandwich	**sendvič od sira** send-wich od seera
a ham sandwich	**sendvič od šunke** send-wich od shoonkeh
a pancake	**palačinku** palach-inkoo
a packet of crisps	**paketić krispsa** pack-et-ich krisp-sa

These are some other snacks you may like to try:

sendvič od budžole send-wich od boojol-eh	a pork sausage sandwich – a speciality
sendvič od čajne kobasice send-wich od chaee-neh kobas-eetseh	a sandwich of smoked sausage
sendvič od dalmatinske šunke send-wich od dalmat-eenskeh shoonkeh	a Parma ham sandwich
sendvič od Gavrilović salame send-wich od gavril-ovich sala-meh	a salami sandwich (Gavrilovic is Yugoslavia's best known salami)

*Men use the first alternative, women the second

sendvič od gušče pastete	a goose paté sandwich
send-wich od *goosh*-cheh pash-tet-eh	
sendvič od livanskog sira	a Serbian cheese sandwich
send-wich od *leevan*-skog *seera*	
sendvič od mortadele	a mortadella sandwich
send-wich od mortad*el*-eh	
sendvič od piletine	a chicken sandwich
send-wich od *peelet*-eeneh	

Chips are not available as snacks. They can only be ordered as part of a meal in a restaurant when you should ask for **'pom frit'.**
[*For other essential expressions, see 'Ordering a drink', p. 80*]

In a restaurant

ESSENTIAL INFORMATION

- The place to ask for:
  RESTORAN [see p. 20]
  You can eat at these places:
  RESTORAN
  BIFE
  (light snacks, alcoholic and soft drinks)
  EKSPRES RESTORAN
  (self-service, available only in large towns)
  GOSTIONA
  (modest restaurant)
  KAVANA
  (ice-creams, cakes, tea, coffee and alcoholic drinks)
  MLIJEČNI RESTORAN
  (dairy bar)
  RIBLJI RESTORAN
  (principally for fish dishes)

- By law, the menus must be displayed outside or in the window:
  and that is the *only* way to judge if a place is right for your needs.

- Self-service restaurants do exist, but most places have waiter
  service.

- Tipping is not obligatory but even where service is included, it is
  customary to tip 10% of the bill.

- Children's portions (**POLA PORCIJE**) are not commonly available, but it may be worth asking.

- Eating times are flexible and vary between 12.00 p.m. to 13.00
  p.m. and 7.00 p.m. to 11.00 p.m.

WHAT TO SAY

May I book a table?	**Mogu li rezervirati jedan stol?**
	mog-oo lee rezair-veer-atee yed-an stol
I've booked a table	**Imam rezervirani stol**
	eem-um rezair-veer-anee stol
A table . . .	**Stol . . .**
	stol . . .
for one	**za jedno**
	za yed-no
for three	**za troje**
	za troy-eh
The menu, please	**Jelovnik, molim**
	yelov-neek mol-im
The fixed-price menu	**Pansionski jelovnik**
	pansion-skee yelov-neek
The tourist menu	**Turistički jelovnik**
	toorist-ich-kee yelov-neek
Today's special menu	**Današnji specijalni jelovnik**
	dan-ashn-yee spetsial-nee yelov-neek
What's this, please?	**Što je ovo, molim?**
[point to the menu]	shto yeh ov-o mol-im
The wine list	**Vinska karta**
	veen-ska karta
A carafe of wine, please	**Bocu vina, molim**
	botsoo veena mol-im
A quarter (25 cc)	**Četvrt litre vina**
	chet-vert leetreh veena
A half (50 cc)	**Pola litre vina**
	pol-a leetreh veena
A glass	**Čašu**
	cha-shoo
A bottle	**Bocu**
	botsoo
A half-bottle	**Pola boce**
	pol-a botseh
A litre	**Litru**
	leet-roo
Red/white/rosé/house wine	**Crnog/bijelog/ružičastog/domaćeg vina**
	tser-nog/bee-yel-og/roosh-ichastog/domach-eg veena

Some more bread, please	**Malo više kruha, molim**
	ma-lo veesheh krooha, mol-im
Some more wine	**Malo više vina**
	ma-lo veesheh veena
Some oil	**Malo ulja**
	ma-lo ool-ya
Some vinegar	**Malo octa**
	ma-lo ots-ta
Some salt	**Malo soli**
	ma-lo sol-ee
Some pepper	**Malo bibera**
	ma-lo beeb-era
Some water	**Malo vode**
	ma-lo vod-eh
How much does that come to?	**Koliko to košta?**
	kol-eeko to koshta
Is service included?	**Da li je servis uračunat?**
	da lee yeh sair-vis oorach-oonat
Where is the toilet, please?	**Gdje je toaleta, molim?**
	gd-yeh yeh twa-leh-ta, mol-im
Miss! [*This does not sound abrupt in Serbo-Croat*]	**Gospodjice!**
	gospoj-yeetseh
Waiter!	**Konobar!**
	kon-obar
The bill, please	**Račun, molim**
	rach-oon mol-im

Key words for courses, as seen on some menus
[*Only ask the question if you want the waiter to remind you of the choice.*]

What have you got in the way of . . .	**Što imate za . . .**
	shto eemat-eh za . . .
STARTERS?	**PREDJELO?**
	pred-ee-yelo
SOUP?	**JUHU?**
	yoo-hoo
EGG DISHES?	**JAJA?**
	ya-ya
FISH?	**RIBU?**
	reeboo
MEAT?	**MESO?**
	meh-so

GAME?	**DIVLJAČ?**
	d*eev*-leeach
FOWL?	**PILETINU?**
	p*eel*et-eenoo
VEGETABLES?	**POVRĆE?**
	pov-*er*cheh
CHEESE?	**SIR?**
	s*eer*
FRUIT?	**VOĆE?**
	v*o*ch-eh
ICE-CREAM?	**SLADOLED**
	sl*a*doh-led
DESSERT?	**DEZERT?**
	dez*ai*rt

UNDERSTANDING THE MENU

- You will find that most menus in Yugoslavia are in one or more European languages and the names of the various dishes will differ all over the country.
- You will find the names of the principal ingredients of most dishes on these pages:

Starters see p.69	Fruit see p. 72
Meat see p. 75	Dessert see p. 62
Fish see p. 77	Cheese see p. 69
Vegetables see p. 73	Ice-cream see p. 64

- Used together with the following list of cooking and menu terms, they should help you to decode the menu.
- These cooking and menu terms are for understanding only – not for speaking aloud.

Cooking and menu terms

banjo marija	bain marie
na dalmatinsku	Dalmatian
dimljeno	smoked
dinstovano	stewed
dobro kuvano⎤	
dobro pečeno ⎦	well done
faširano	minced
filovano	stuffed
frigano	fried

garnirano	garnished
na gradele	grilled
gusta juha	thick soup
hladno	cold
juha	broth
sa kiselim vrhnjem	with sour cream
kuvano	boiled
kuvano u pari	steamed
na maslu	with butter
meso u hladetini	meat in aspic jelly
minestrun	vegetable soup
mljeveno	ground
sa mušulama	with mussels
pasirano	creamed
u peć	in the oven
pečeno	roast
pirjano (podušeno)	poached
pire	purée
polupečeno	rare
u prosulju	in the frying pan
punjeno	stuffed
na puteru	with butter
prženo	fried
ragu	stew
na ražnju	on the spit
na roštilju	grilled
seckano	diced
slatko/kiselo	sweet/sour
srednje pečeno	medium done
ukiseljeno (meso/riba)	marinated (meat/fish)
u umaku	with sauce
na žaru	grilled on charcoal

Further words to help you understand the menu

bakalar	cod (dried)
barbuni	red mullet
bubrezi	kidneys
ćevapčići	kebab of minced meat
djuveč	a vegetable dish of tomatoes with peppers and aubergines, sometimes part of a meat stew – the menu will specify

dvopek u kremi	trifle
faširano meso	minced meat
fazan	pheasant
file steak	fillet steak
gavuni	sprats
girice	small Adriatic fish (sprats)
golub	pigeon
govedje pečenje	roast beef
janjeće pečenje	roast lamb
jarebica	partridge
jastog	lobster
jegulje	eels
jetra	liver
jezik	tongue
juha od paradajza	tomato soup
kobasice	sausages
kolač	cake
krezle	sweetbreads
kunić	rabbit
lignji	squid
marinirane gljive	marinated mushrooms
mozak	brain
musaka	moussaka: layers of minced meat and sliced aubergines with a topping of eggs and sour milk.
omleti	omelets
palačinke	pancakes
patka	duck
piletina na ražnju	chicken on the spit
piletina pržena	fried chicken
piletina pohana	chicken fried in breadcrumbs
punjena jaja	stuffed eggs
punjeni patlidžan	stuffed aubergines
punjeni paradajz	stuffed tomatoes
punjene paprike	stuffed peppers in tomato sauce
punjene tikvice	stuffed courgettes
puran	turkey
rak	crab
razne salate	various salads
razni sladoledi	various ice-creams
ražnjići	pieces of pork/veal on skewers – shish kebab

riblja juha	fish soup
rižot	risotto
salama	salami
sarma	stuffed and pickled cabbage leaves in tomato sauce
škampi na žaru	scampi grilled on charcoal
slanina	bacon
srce	heart
šunka	ham
svinjska glava	pig's head
svinjska koljenica	pig's trotters
svinjsko pečenje	roast pork
teleće pečenje	roast veal
zelena menestra	green leaf soup with ham
zec (divlji)	hare (wild)
zubatac	a large delicately flavoured fish (dentex)

Health

ESSENTIAL INFORMATION

- The medical care of British nationals in Yugoslavia is regulated by a convention signed by the two countries. British nationals have the right to free medical care on production of a valid travel document and on payment of a minimal fee.
- It is, however, also advisable to purchase a medical insurance policy through a travel agent, a broker or a motoring organization.
- Take your own 'first line' first aid kit with you.
- For minor disorders and treatment at a chemist's, see. p. 42.
- For finding your way to a doctor, dentist and chemist, see p. 20.
- Once in Yugoslavia decide on a definite plan of action in case of serious illness: communicate your problem to a near neighbour, the receptionist or someone you see regularly. You are then dependent on that person helping you obtain treatment.

WHAT'S THE MATTER?

I have a pain in my . . .	Boli me . . .
	bol-ee meh . . .
ankle	članak
	chl*a*n-ak
arm	ruka
	r*oo*ka
back	ledja
	le*j*-ah
bladder	mjehur
	m-yeh-hoor
bowels	crijeva
	tsree-yeh-va
breast	grudi
	gr*oo*dee
chest	prsa
	per-sa
ear	uho
	oo-ho
eye	oko
	o-ko

foot	**stopalo**
	stop-alo
head	**glava**
	gla-va
heel	**peta**
	peh-ta
jaw	**vilica**
	veelee-tsa
kidney	**bubreg**
	boob-reg
leg	**noga**
	nog-a
lungs	**pluća**
	plooch-ah
neck	**vrat**
	ver-at
penis	**penis**
	peh-nis
shoulder	**rame**
	ra-meh
stomach (abdomen)	**stomak**
	stomach
testicle	**mudo**
	moodo
throat	**grlo**
	ger-lo
vagina	**vagina**
	vag-eena
wrist	**ručni zglavak**
	rooch-nee z-glav-ak
I have a pain here [point]	**Boli me ovdje**
	bol-ee meh ovd-yeh
I have toothache	**Boli me zub**
	bol-ee meh zoob
I have broken . . .	**Slomio/slomila* sam . . .**
	slom-ee-o/slom-eela sum . . .
my dentures	**moju protezu**
	moyoo protez-oo
my glasses	**moje naočale**
	moyeh now-cha-leh

*Men use the first alternative, women the second

I have lost . . .	**Izgubio/izgubila* sam . . .** *eez*-goobee-o/*eez*-goobee-la sum . .
my contact lenses	**moja kontaktna stakla** m*o*ya c*o*ntact-na st*a*k-la
a filling	**plombu** pl*o*m-boo
My child is ill	**Moje je dijete bolesno** m*o*yeh yeh dee-*y*et-eh b*o*l-esno
He/she has a pain in his/her . . .	**Boli ga/boli je . . .** b*o*l-ee ga/b*o*l-ee yeh . . .
ankle [*see list above*]	**članak** chl*a*n-ak

How bad is it?

I'm ill	**Ja se osjećam bolestan/bolesna*** ya seh *o*s-yech-am b*o*l-estan/ b*o*l-esna
It's urgent	**Hitno je** h*ee*t-no yeh
It's serious	**Ozbiljno je** *o*z-beel-no yeh
It's not serious	**Nije ozbiljno** n*ee*-yeh *o*z-beel-no
It hurts	**Boli** b*o*l-ee
It hurts a lot	**Boli puno** b*o*l-ee p*oo*no
It doesn't hurt much	**Ne boli puno** neh b*o*l-ee p*oo*no
The pain occurs . . .	**Bol se ponavlja redovito . . .** bohl seh p*o*n-avl-ya red*o*v-eeto . . .
every quarter of an hour	**svako četvrt sata** sv*a*k-o ch*e*tvert s*a*-ta
every half an hour	**svako pola sata** sv*a*k-o p*o*l-a s*a*-ta
every hour	**svaki sat** sv*a*k-ee s*a*ht
every day	**svaki dan** sv*a*k-ee d*u*n
most of the time	**većinom vremena** vech*ee*n-om vr*e*m-ena

*Men use the first alternative, women the second

I've had it for . . .	**Boli me već ima . . .** b*o*l-ee meh v*e*ch *ee*ma . . .
one hour/one day	**jedan sat/jedan dan** y*e*d-an s*a*ht/y*e*d-an d*u*n
two hours/two days	**dva sata/dva dana** dva s*a*-ta/dva d*a*-na
It's a . . .	**To je . . .** toh yeh . . .
sharp pain	**jaka bol** y*a*k-a bohl
dull ache	**mrtva bol** m*e*rt-va bohl
nagging pain	**uporna bol** *oo*por-na bohl
I feel dizzy	**Vrti mi se u glavi** v*e*r-tee mee seh oo gl*a*-vee
I feel sick	**Zlo mi je** zlo mee yeh
I feel weak	**Slabo mi je** sl*a*-bo mee yeh
I feel feverish	**Grozničav sam** gr*o*z-neechav sum

Already under treatment for something else?

I take . . . regularly [*show*]	**Uzimam redovito . . .** *oo*zee-mum red*o*v-eetoh . . .
this medicine	**ovaj lijek** *o*v-oy l*ee*-yek
these pills	**ove pilule** *o*v-eh p*ee*lool-eh
I have . . .	**Bolujem od . . .** b*o*loo-yem od . . .
a heart condition	**srca** s*e*r-tsa
haemorrhoids	**hemoroida** hem-or*o*yda
rheumatism	**reumatizma** reh-oomat-*ee*zma

I am . . .	Ja sam . . .
	ya sum . . .
diabetic	**dijabetičar**
	dee-*a*-bet-eechar
asthmatic	**astmatičar**
	asm*a*t-eechar
pregnant	**očekujem bebu**
	ochek-ooyem beb-oo
I'm allergic to penicillin	**Ja sam alergičan/alergična* na penicilin**
	ya sum *a*lairg-ichan/*a*lairg-ich-na na penitsil-*ee*noo

Other essential expressions

Please can you help?	**Molim, možete li pomoći?**
	m*o*lim mosh-et-eh lee p*o*m-ochee
A doctor, please	**Doktora, molim**
	doctora m*o*l-im
A dentist	**Zubara**
	z*oo*bara
I don't speak Serbo-Croat	**Ne govorim srpsko-hrvatski**
	neh g*o*v-orim s*e*rpsko-h*e*rvatskee
What time does . . .	**U koliko sati . . .**
	oo k*o*l-eeko s*a*-tee . . .
the doctor open?	**doktor počimje raditi?**
	d*o*ctor p*o*chem-yeh r*a*d-eetee
the dentist open?	**zubar počimje raditi?**
	z*oo*bar p*o*cheem-yeh r*a*d-eetee

From the doctor: key sentences to understand

Take this . . .	**Uzmite ovo . . .**
	*oo*z-meet-eh ov-o . . .
every day/hour	**svaki dan/svaki sat**
	sv*a*k-ee dun/sv*a*k-ee s*a*ht
Stay in bed	**Ostanite u krevetu**
	*o*stan-eet-eh oo krev-et-oo
Don't travel . . .	**Nemoj te putovati . . .**
	nem-oy teh pootov-atee . . .
for . . . days/weeks	**za . . . dana/sedmice**
	za . . . d*a*-na/sed-mee-tseh
You must go to hospital	**Treba da idete u bolnicu**
	treb-a da *ee*d-et-eh oo b*o*lnee-tsoo

*Men use the first alternative, women the second

Problems: complaints, loss, theft

ESSENTIAL INFORMATION

- Problems with:
  camping facilities, see p. 36
  household appliances, see p. 38
  health, see p. 92
  the car, see p. 106
- If the worst comes to the worst, find the police station. To ask the way, see p. 20.
- Look for:
  MILICIJA (police)
  SAOBRAĆAJNA MILICIJA (traffic police)
  POGRANIČNA MILICIJA (frontier police)
  LUČKA KAPETANIJA (port authority)
- If you lose your passport, go to the nearest British Consulate.
- In an emergency dial 94 for an ambulance, 93 for the fire brigade and 92 for the police.

COMPLAINTS

I bought this ...	**Kupio sam ovo ...**
	k*oo*pee-o sum *ov*-o ...
today	**danas**
	d*a*-nus
yesterday	**jučer**
	y*oo*ch-er
on Monday [see p. 130]	**u ponedjeljak**
	oo pon-*e*d-yel-yak
It's no good	**Nije dobro**
	n*ee*-yeh d*o*b-ro
Look	**Pogledajte**
	p*o*gleh-daee-teh
Here [point]	**Ovdje**
	*o*vd-yeh
Can you ...	**Možete li ...**
	m*o*sh-et-eh lee ...
change it?	**promijenuti?**
	promee-y*e*n-ootee
mend it?	**popraviti?**
	poprav-eetee

Here's the receipt	**Ovdje je priznanica**
	ovd-yeh yeh preeznan-eetsa
Can I have a refund?	**Mogu li dobiti novac natrag?**
	mog-oo lee dob-eetee novats natrag
Can I see the manager?	**Mogu li da vidim direktora?**
	mog-oo lee da veedeem deerectora

Loss
[*See also 'Theft' below: the lists are interchangeable*]

I have lost . . .	**Izgubio/izgubila sam* . . .**
	eez-goobee-o/eez-goobee-la sum . .
my bag	**moju tašnu**
	moyoo tashnoo
my bracelet	**moju narukvicu**
	moyoo na-rook-veetsoo
my camera	**moj fotoaparat**
	moy photo-aparat
my car keys	**ključeve mojih kola**
	klee-yooch-eh-veh moyeeh kola
my car logbook	**saobraćajnu knijižicu**
	sa-obracha-eenoo kn-yee-shee-tsoo
my driving licence	**moju vozačku dozvolu**
	moy-oo vozach-koo doz-vol-oo
my insurance certificate	**moju potvrdu osiguranja**
	moy-oo pot-ver-doo oseegoo-ran-ya
my jewellery	**moje dragulje**
	moy-eh drag-ool-yeh
everything	**sve**
	sveh

Theft
[*See also 'Loss' above: the lists are interchangeable*]

Someone has stolen . . .	**Ukrali su mi . . .**
	ookra-lee soo mee . . .
my car	**moja kola**
	moya kola
my car radio	**radio mojih kola**
	ra-dio moyeeh kola

*Men use the first alternative, women the second

my money	**moj novac**
	moy nov-ats
my necklace	**moju ogrlicu**
	moy-oo og-erlee-tsoo
my passport	**moj pasoš**
	moy pas-osh
my radio	**moj radio**
	moy ra-dio
my tickets	**moje karte**
	moy-eh karteh
my travellers' cheques	**moje putne čekove**
	moy-eh poot-neh chek-oveh
my wallet	**moj novčanik**
	moy nov-chan-ik
my watch	**moj sat**
	moy saht
my luggage	**moju prtljagu**
	moy-oo pertl-ya-goo

LIKELY REACTIONS: key words to understand

Wait	**Počekajte**
	poch-ek-ah-eeteh
When?	**Kada?**
	ka-da
Where?	**Gdje?**
	gd-yeh
Name?	**Ime?**
	eemeh
Address?	**Adresa?**
	adresa
I can't help you	**Ne mogu vam pomoći**
	neh mog-oo vum pom-ochee
Nothing to do with me	**To nije moja stvar**
	toh nee-yeh moya stvar

The post office

ESSENTIAL INFORMATION

- To find a post office, see p. 20.
- Key words to look for **POŠTA, TELEGRAF I TELEFON**
- Look for this sign:

- For stamps look for the word **MARKE** on a post office counter.
- Stamps are also sold at tobacconists, newsagents and stationers.
- Letter boxes are yellow, and fixed to the walls.
- For post-restante, you should show your passport at the counter marked **POSTE RESTANTE**: a small fee is usually payable.

WHAT TO SAY

To England, please
Za Englesku, molim
za en-gles-koo mol-im

[*Hand letters, cards or parcels over the counter*]

To Australia
Za Australiju
za *ah*-oostralee-yoo

To the United States
za Ameriku

[*For other countries see p. 134*] za amerik-oo

How much is . . .	Koliko košta . . .
	kol-eeko koshta . . .
this parcel (to Canada)?	**ovaj paket (za Kanadu)?**
	ov-aee pack-et (za kanadoo)
a letter (to Australia)?	**pismo (za Australiju)?**
	peesmo (za ah-oostralee-yoo)
a postcard (to England)?	**dopisnica (za Englesku)?**
	dop-eesneetsa (za en-gles-koo)
Airmail	**Avionom**
	avee-onom
Surface mail	**Običnom poštom**
	obeech-nom posh-tom
One stamp, please	**Jednu marku, molim**
	yed-noo markoo mol-im
Two stamps	**Dvije marke**
	dvee-yeh markeh
One (2) dinar stamp	**Jednu marku od (dva) dinara**
	yed-noo markoo od (dva) deena-ra
I'd like to send a telegram	**Želim da pošaljem telegram**
	shel-im da poshal-yem telegram

Telephoning

ESSENTIAL INFORMATION

- Unless you read and speak Serbo-Croat well, it's best not to make phone calls by yourself. Go to a post office and write the town and number you want on a piece of paper. Add 'COLLECT CALL' if you want a person-to-person call or PCV if you want to reverse the charges.
- Telephones are usually attached to the walls of public buildings in rectangular brick red boxes – these are for local calls only. Insert the dinar coins as required in the correct slot and dial when the red light appears. Speak when you hear your caller. If you don't get through press down the receiver cradle to recover your money.
- The code for the UK is 9944 followed by the UK subscriber's own telephone number. Calls to the USA have to go through the operator.
- You can ask at your local post office for a brochure on phoning England from abroad.

WHAT TO SAY

Where can I make a telephone call? **Gdje mogu da telefoniram?**
gd-yeh mog-oo da telephon-eeram

Local/abroad **Za unutrašnjost/inozemstvo**
za oonoo-trashn-yost/eenozems-tvo

I'd like this number . . . **Želim ovaj broj . . .**
[show number] shel-im ov-eey broy . . .

in England **za Englesku**
za en-gles-koo

in Canada **za Kanadu**
za kanadoo

in the USA **za Ameriku**
[For other countries, p. 134] za omerikoo

Can you dial it for me, please? **Možete li vi nazvati za mene, molim?**
mosh-et-eh lee vee naz-va-tee za meh-neh mol-im

How much is it? **Koliko košta?**
kol-eeko koshta

Hello

May I speak to . . . ?

Extension . . .

I'm sorry, I don't speak
   Serbo-Croat

Do you speak English?

Thank you, I'll phone back

Goodbye

Halo/molim
ha-lo/mol-im

Mogu li govoriti sa . . . ?
mog-oo lee gov-oree-tee sa . . .

Lokal . . .
local . . .

Žao mi je, ali ne govorim
   srpsko-hrvatski
sha-o mee yeh ah-lee neh gov-oreem
   serpsko-hervatskee

Govorite li vi engleski?
gov-oree-teh lee vee en-gleskee

Hvala, nazvat ću kasnije
fa-la naz-vat choo kasnee-yeh

Zbogom
zbog-om

LIKELY REACTIONS

That's 10 dinars

Cabin number (3)
[For numbers, see p. 125]

Don't hang up

I'm trying to connect you

You're through

There's a delay

I'll try again

To košta sto pedeset dinara
to koshta sto peh-deh-set deen-ara

Govornica broj (tri)
govor-neetsa broy (tree)

Nemojte prekinuti
nem-oy-teh prek-eenoo-tee

Pokušavam da vas spojim
pokoosh-avum da vus spoy-im

Imate vezu
eema-teh vez-oo

Ima zakašnjenja
eema zakashnee-yen-ya

Pokušat ću kasnije ponovo
pokoosh-at choo kasnee-yeh
   po-no-vo

Changing cheques and money

ESSENTIAL INFORMATION

- Finding your way to a bank or change bureau, see p. 20.
- Look for these words on buildings:
  BANKA (bank)
  MJENJAČNICA (money changed)
  NARODNA BANKA (national bank)
  TURISTIČKA AGENCIJA (most travel agencies will change money)
- Money can also be changed at some post offices. It is illegal to change foreign currency other than in official exchange offices. Avoid all approaches to change money – particularly on trains.
- To cash your own normal cheques, exactly as at home, use your banker's card where you see the Eurocheque sign. Write in English, in pounds.
- Exchange rate information might show the pound as:
  L, GB, VB
- Have your passport handy.

WHAT TO SAY

I'd like to cash ...	**Želim da promjenim ...**
	shel-im da prom-yen-im ...
this travellers' cheque	**ovaj putni ček**
	ov-aee poot-nee check
these travellers' cheques	**ove putne čekove**
	ov-eh poot-neh check-oveh
this cheque	**ovaj ček**
	ov-aee check
I'd like to change this into dinars	**Želim da promjenim ovo u dinare**
	shel-im da prom-yen-im ov-o oo deen-areh
Here's ...	**Izvolite ...**
	eez-vol-eeteh ...
my banker's card	**moju bankarsku potvrdu**
	moy-oo bankar-skoo pot-ver-doo
my passport	**moj pasoš**
	moy pas-osh

For excursions into neighbouring countries

I'd like to change this . . .	**Želim da promjenim ovo . . .**
[*show banknotes*]	shel-im da prom-yen-im ov-o . . .
into Austrian schillings	**u austrijske šilinge**
	oo *ah*-oos-tree-skeh sh*ee*-leen-geh
into Hungarian forint	**u madžarske forinte**
	oo m*a*d-jar-skeh for*ee*n-teh
into Rumanian leu	**u rumunjske leje**
	oo r*oo*moon-skeh l*e*h-yeh
into Bulgarian lev	**u bugarske leve**
	oo b*oo*gar-skeh l*e*v-eh
into Italian lira	**u talijanske lire**
	oo tal*ee*-yan-skeh l*ee*reh
into Greek drachma	**u grčke drahme**
	oo g*e*rch-keh dr*a*-hmeh
into Albanian lek	**u albanske leke**
	oo *a*lban-skeh lek-eh
What's the rate of exchange?	**Kakav je kurs?**
	k*a*-kav yeh k*oo*rs

LIKELY REACTIONS

Passport, please	**Pasoš, molim**
	p*a*s-osh m*o*l-im
Sign here	**Potpišite se ovdje**
	pot-p*ee*sh-eeteh seh *o*vd-yeh
Your banker's card, please	**Vašu bankarsku potvrdu, molim**
	v*a*shoo b*a*nkar-skoo pot-ver-doo m*o*l-im
Go to the cash desk	**Izvolite na kasu**
	*ee*z-vol-eeteh na k*a*-soo

Car travel

ESSENTIAL INFORMATION

- Finding a filling station or garage, see p. 20.
- Grades of petrol:
  NORMAL (86 octane)
  MJEŠAVINA (mixed)
  SUPER (98 octane)
  NAFTA/DIZL (gas oil/diesel)
- 1 gallon is about 4½ litres (accurate enough up to 6 gallons).
- For general repairs, look for the sign
  AUTOMEHANIKA
  Other garages with the proprietor's name in front of the sign
  SERVIS undertake general repair work.
- Opening times: 6.00 a.m. – 12.00 p.m.
- You will find 24-hour service stations along the main roads.
- The Yugoslav Automobile Association (AMSJ) runs some 120 assistance/information bases which are manned by mechanics and open between 8.00 a.m. and 8.00 p.m. Some of these stations still have individual telephone numbers, but many of them can be contacted on 987.
- Members of foreign motoring and touring clubs may get free legal advice from lawyers associated with the Yugoslav AA (particularly applicable in larger towns).
- Unfamiliar road signs and warnings, see p. 121.

WHAT TO SAY
[*For numbers, see p. 125*]

(9) litres of . . .	**(Devet) litara . . .** deh-vet l*ee*t-ara . . .
(150) dinars of . . .	**(Sto pedeset) dinara . . .** sto peh-deh-set d*ee*n-ara . . .
standard	**normala** norm*a*l-ah
premium	**supera** s*o*oper-ah
diesel	**mješavine/nafte** mee-yesha-veeneh/n*a*fteh
Fill it up, please	**Napunite, molim** n*a*poo-neeteh mol-im

Will you check . . .	**Molim vas provjerite . . .**
	m*o*l-im vus pr*o*v-yair-eeteh **. . .**
the oil?	**ulje?**
	*oo*l-yeh
the battery?	**akumulator?**
	akoomool*a*-tor
the radiator?	**radijator?**
	rad-*ya*-tor
the tyres?	**gume?**
	g*oo*meh
I've run out of petrol	**Ostao sam bez benzine**
	*o*sta-o sum b*e*nzeeneh
Can I borrow a can, please?	**Možete li mi posuditi kantu, molim**
	mosh-et-eh lee mee pos-*oo*deet-ee kantoo m*o*l-im
My car has broken down	**Kola su mi se pokvarila**
	k*o*la soo mee seh pok-v*a*r-eela
My car won't start	**Ne mogu da pokrenem kola**
	neh m*o*g-oo da p*o*kreh-nem kola
I've had an accident	**Dogodila mi se nesreća**
	do-g*o*-dee-la mee seh n*e*s-recha
I've lost my car keys	**Izgubio sam ključeve od kola**
	eez-goobee-o sum klee-yoo-cheh-veh od kola
My car is . . .	**moja su kola . . .**
	m*o*ya soo kola **. . .**
two kilometres away	**na dva kilometra odavle**
	na dva keel*o*-met-ra *o*d-av-leh
three kilometres away	**na tri kilometra odavle**
	na tree keel*o*-met-ra *o*d-av-leh
Can you help me, please?	**Možete li mi pomoći, molim vas?**
	mosh-et-eh lee mee p*o*m-ochee m*o*l-im vus
Do you do repairs?	**Da li pravite popravke?**
	da lee pr*a*-veeteh p*o*p-rav-keh
I have a puncture	**Imam probušenu gumu**
	*ee*m-am pr*o*-booshenoo g*oo*moo
I have a broken windscreen	**Imam razbijeno predje staklo**
	*ee*m-am raz-bee-*ye*n-o pred-yeh st*a*klo
I think the problem is here . . . [point]	**Mislim da je problem ovdje . . .**
	m*ee*slim da yeh pr*o*blem *o*vd-yeh **. . .**

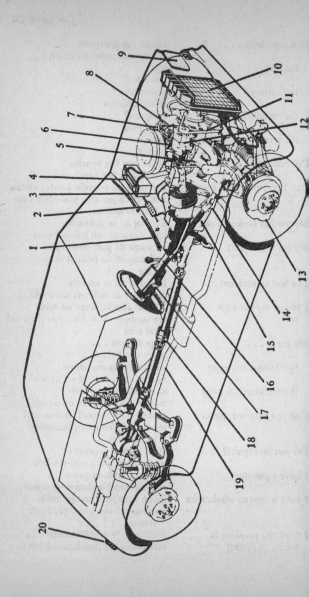

1 windscreen wipers	**brisači** brees*ach*-ee	11 fan belt	**remen ventilatora** reh-men venteela-*tora*
2 fuses	**osigurači** *ose*egoo-rachee	12 generator	**generator** ghenerat-*or*
3 heater	**grijač** gree-*yach*	13 brakes	**kočnica** koch-nee-tsa
4 battery	**akumulator** akoomoola-*tor*	14 clutch	**mjenjač** *mee*-yen-yach
5 engine	**motor** *mo*-tor	15 gear box	**kutija mjenjača** kootee-ya m-yen-ya-cha
6 fuel pump	**pumpa benzina** *poompa* benzeeneh	16 steering	**upravljanje** *oopravl*-yan-yeh
7 starter motor	**startni motor** *start*-nee *mo*-tor	17 ignition	**paljenje** *pal*-yen-yeh
8 carburettor	**karburator** kar-boor*a*-tor.	18 transmission	**prenos** preh-nos
9 lights	**fare** fa-reh	19 exhaust	**ispusna cijev** *ees*-poos-na tsee-yev
10 radiator	**radijator** radee-*ya*-tor	20 indicators	**žmigavci** shm*eeg*-av-tsee

I don't know what's wrong	**Ne znam što nije u redu**
	neh znam shto nee-yeh oo red-oo
Can you ...	**Možete li vi ...**
	mosh-et-eh lee vee ...
repair the fault?	**popraviti kvar?**
	pop-rav-eetee kvar
come and look?	**doći i pogledati?**
	doh-chee ee pogleh-da-tee
estimate the cost?	**procijeniti?**
	pro-tsee-yeh-neetee
write it down?	**napisati?**
	napees-atee
Do you accept these coupons?	**Da li primate ove kupone?**
	da lee preemat-eh ov-eh coupon-eh
How long will the repair take?	**Koliko će trebati vremena za popravak?**
	kol-eeko cheh treb-atee vrem-ena za pop-ra-vak
When will the car be ready?	**Kada će kola biti gotova?**
	ka-da cheh kola beetee got-ov-ah
Can I see the bill?	**Mogu li da vidim račun?**
	mog-oo lee da veedeem rach-oon
This is my insurance document	**Ovo je moja isprava osiguranja**
	ov-o yeh moya eesp-rava oseegooran-ya

HIRING A CAR

Can I hire a car?	**Mogu li da iznajmim kola?**
	mog-oo lee da eez-naee-mim kola
I need a car ...	**Trebaju mi kola ...**
	treb-ayoo mee kola ...
for two people	**za dvije osobe**
	za dvee-yeh os-obeh
for five people	**za pet osoba**
	za pet os-oba
for one day	**za jedan dan**
	za yed-an dun
for five days	**za pet dana**
	za pet dun-ah
for a week	**za jednu nedjelju**
	za yed-noo ned-yel-yoo

Can you write down . . . **Možete li napisati . . .**
mosh-et-eh lee nap*ee*s-atee . . .

the deposit to pay? **kolika je kaucija?**
kol-*ee*ka yeh c*ow*-tsee-ya

the charge per kilometre? **koliko košta po kilometru?**
kol-*ee*ko koshta po keel*o*-metroo

the daily charge? **koliko košta na dan?**
kol-*ee*ko koshta na d*u*n

the cost of insurance? **koliko košta osiguranje?**
kol-*ee*ko koshta oseegoo-ran-yeh

Can I leave it in (Split)? **Mogu li da ih ostavim (Split)?**
m*o*g-oo lee da ee *o*sta-veem
(spl*ee*t)

What documents do I need? **Koji dokumenti su mi potrebni?**
koyee doh-k*oo*-mentee soo mee
pot-reb-nee

LIKELY REACTIONS

I don't do repairs **Ne vršim popravke**
neh v*e*r-sheem poprav-keh

Where is your car? **Gdje su vaša kola?**
gd-yeh soo v*a*sha k*o*la

What make is it? **Koja je marka Vaših kola?**
k*o*ya yeh m*a*rka v*a*sh-eeh k*o*la

Come back tomorrow/on **Povratite se sutra/u ponedjeljak**
Monday pov-r*a*t-eeteh seh s*oo*tra/oo
[For days of the week, p. 130] poned-yel-yak

I don't hire cars **Ne iznajmivam kola**
neh eez-n*a*ee-meev-am k*o*la

Your driving licence, please **Vašu vozačku dozvolu, molim**
vash-oo voz-ach-koo dozvol-oo

The mileage is unlimited **Kilometraža je neograničena**
keelo-metr*a*sh-ah yeh neh
neh-ogr*a*n-eechena

Public transport

ESSENTIAL INFORMATION

- Finding the way to the bus station, a bus stop, a tram stop, the railway station and a taxi rank, see p. 20.
- Remember that queuing for buses is unheard of.
- You can hail a taxi as you would normally but it's best to go to a taxi rank.
- Types of train:
  brzi vlak   (stops at principal stations)
  expresni vlak (stops at principal stations; a supplement is payable)
  putnički vlak (stops at all stations)
  poslovni vlak (commuter train)
- Key words on signs [see also p. 121]
  ŽELJEZNIČKA STANICA (railway station)
  PRODAJA KARTA (tickets, ticket office)
  ULAZ (entrance)
  ZABRANJENO JE (forbidden)
  ULAZ (entrance, for buses)
  PERON (platform)
  URED ZA INFORMACIJE (information, information office)
  ČEKAONICA (waiting room)
  ŽTP JŽ (initials for Yugoslav railways)
  IZLAZ (exit)
  GARDEROBA (left luggage)
  AUTOBUSNA STANICA (bus stop)
  RED VOŽNJE (timetable)

WHAT TO SAY

Where does the train for (Belgrade) leave from?

Odakle polazi vlak za (Beograd)?
od-akleh pol-azee vlak za (beh-ograd)

At what time does the train leave for (Belgrade)?

U koliko sati polazi vlak za Beograd?
oo kol-eeko sa-tee pol-azee vlak za (beh-ograd)

At what time does the train arrive in (Belgrade)?

U koliko sati stiže vlak u (Beograd)?
oo kol-eeko sa-tee steesh-eh vlak oo (beh-ograd)

[For times, see p. 128]

this train for (Belgrade)?	**Da li je ovo vlak za (Beograd)?**
	da lee yeh ov-o vlak za (beh-ograd)?
Where does the bus for (Split) leave from?	**Odakle polazi autobus za (Split)?**
	od-akleh pol-azee ah-ooto-boos za (spleet)?
At what time does the bus leave for (Split)?	**U koliko sati polazi autobus za (Split)?**
	oo kol-eeko sa-tee pol-azee ah-ooto-boos za (spleet)?
At what time does the bus arrive at (Split)?	**U koliko sati stiže autobus u (Split)?**
	oo kol-eeko sa-tee stee-sheh ah-ooto-boos oo (spleet)?
Is this the bus for (Split)?	**Da li je ovo autobus za (Split)?**
	da lee yeh ov-o ah-ooto-boos za (spleet)?
Do I have to change?	**Moram li da presjedim?**
	mor-am lee da pres-yeh-dim
Where does . . . leave from?	**Odakle polazi . . .**
	od-akleh pol-azee . . .
the bus	**autobus**
	ah-ooto-boos
the train	**vlak**
	vlak
the underground	**podzemna željeznica**
	pod-zem-na shel-yeznee-tsa
for the airport	**za aerodrom**
	za ah-airodrom
for the cathedral	**za katedralu**
	za kat-edral-oo
for the beach	**za plažu**
	za plash-oo
for the market place	**za trg**
	za terg
for the railway station	**željezničku stanicu**
	shel-yez-neech-koo stan-eetsoo
for the town centre	**za centar grada**
	za tsen-tar grad-a
for the St Blase church	**za crkvu Svetog Vlaha**
	za tserk-voo svet-og vla-ha
for the swimming pool	**za bazen**
	za baz-eb

Is this . . .

Da li je ovo . . .
da lee yeh *ov*-o **. . .**

the bus for the market place?

autobus za trg
*a*h-ooto-boos za t*e*rg

the tram for the railway station?

tramvaj za željezničku stanicu
tram-vaee za sh*e*l-yez-neech-koo stan-eetsoo

Where can I get a taxi?

Gdje mogu uzeti taksi?
gd-yeh m*o*g-oo *oo*zet-ee t*a*xi?

Can you put me off at the right stop, please?

Hoćete li mi reći kad treba da se iskrcam, molim vas?
h*o*ch-et-eh lee mee rech-ee kad tr*e*b ah da seh is-k*e*r-tsam mol-im vus

Can I book a seat?

Mogu li rezervirati jedno mjesto?
m*o*g-oo lee rezairv-*ee*r-atee yed-no m-y*e*sto

A single

Jednosmjernu kartu
yed-n*o*-smee-yair-noo kartoo

A return

Jednu povratnu kartu
yed-noo povrat-noo kartoo

First class

Prvi razred
p*e*r-vee r*a*z-red

Second class

Drugi razred
dr*oo*-ghee r*a*z-red

One adult

Za jednu osobu
za yed-noo *o*s-oboo

Two adults

Za dvije osobe
za dv*ee*-yeh *o*s-obeh

and one child

i jedno dijete
ee yed-no dee-yet-eh

and two children

i dvoje djece
ee dv*o*yeh dee-yetseh

How much is it?

Koliko košta?
k*o*l-eeko k*o*shta

LIKELY REACTIONS

Over there	**Tamo**
	ta-mo
Here	**Ovdje**
	ovd-yeh
Platform (1)	**Peron broj (jedan)**
	peh-ron broy (yed-an)
At 16.00	**U šesnaest**
[For times, see p. 128]	oo shehst-na-est
Change at (Sarajevo)	**Presjedajte u (Sarajevu)**
	pres-yed-aeeteh oo (sarayevoo)
Change at (the town hall)	**Presjedajte (kod gradske općine)**
	pres-yed-aeeteh (kod grat-skeh op-cheeneh)
This is your stop	**Ovo je vaša stanica**
	ov-o yeh vasha stan-eetsa
There's only first class	**Ima samo prvi razred**
	eema sa-mo per-vee raz-red
There's a supplement	**Ima dodatak**
	eema dodat-ak

Leisure

ESSENTIAL INFORMATION

- Finding the way to a place of entertainment, see p. 20.
- For times of day see p. 128.
- Important signs, see p. 121.

WHAT TO SAY

At what time does . . . open?	**U koliko sati se otvara . . .** oo kol-eeko sa-tee seh otva-ra . . .
the art gallery	**umjetnička galerija?** oom-yet-neech-ka galaireeya
the botanical garden	**botanički vrt?** bot-aneech-kee vert
the cinema	**kino?** keeno
the concert hall	**koncertna dvorana?** kontsairt-na dvora-na
the disco	**disko?** disko
the museum	**muzej?** mooz-ay
the night club	**noćni lokal?** noch-nee lok-al
the sports stadium	**stadion?** sta-dee-on
the swimming pool	**bazen?** baz-en
the theatre	**pozorište?** poz-orish-teh
the zoo	**zoološki vrt?** zool-osh-kee vert
At what time does . . . close?	**U koliko sati se zatvara . . .** oo kol-eeko sa-tee seh zatva-ra . . .
the art gallery [see above list]	**umjetnička galerija?** oom-yet-neech-ka galaireeya

At what time does . . . start?	Kada počimje . . .
	ka-da pocheem-yeh . . .
the cabaret	kabaret?
	kabaret
the concert	koncert?
	kon-tsairt
the film	film?
	film
the match	utakmica?
	ootak-meetsa
the play	drama?
	drama
the race	trka?
	ter-ka
How much is it . . .	Koliko košta . . .
	kol-eeko koshta . . .
for an adult?	za osobu?
	za os-oboo
for a child?	za dijete?
	za dee-yet-eh
Two adults, please	Dvije osobe, molim
	dvee-yeh os-obeh mol-im
Three children, please	Troje djece, molim
[State price, if there's a choice]	tro-yeh dee-yet-seh mol-im
Stalls/circle	Parter/balkon
	par-tair/balkon
Do you have . . .	Imate li . . .
	eemat-eh lee . . .
a programme?	program?
	pro-gram
a guide book?	vodiča?
	vod-eecha
Where's the toilet, please?	Gdje je toaleta, molim?
	gd-yeh yeh twa-leh-ta mol-im
Where's the cloakroom?	Gdje je garderoba?
	gd-yeh yeh gardeh-roba
I'd like lessons in . . .	Želio/željela* bih lekcije . . .
	shel-yo/shel-yel-ah beeh
	lek-tsee-yeh . . .
skiing	skijanja
	ski-yan-ya

*Men use the first alternative, women the second

I'd like lessons in . . .	**Želio/željela* bih lekcije . . .** shel-yo/shel-yel-ah beeh lek-tsee-yeh . . .
sailing	**jedrenja** yedren-ya
water skiing	**skijanja na moru** ski-yan-ya na moroo
sub-aqua diving	**ronjenja** ron-yen-ya
Can I hire . . .	**Htio/htjela* bih unajmiti . . .** h-tee-o/ht-yel-ah beeh oonaee-meetee . . .
a boat?	**čamac?** cham-ats
a fishing rod?	**trsku za ribarenje?** ter-skoo za reeba-renyeh
a deckchair?	**ležaljku?** lesh-alkoo
a sun umbrella?	**suncobran?** soon-tsobrun
the necessary equipment?	**potrebnu opremu?** pot-reb-noo oprem-oo
How much is it . . .	**Koliko košta . . .** kol-eeko koshta . . .
per day/per hour?	**na dan/na sat?** na dun/na sat
Do I need a licence?	**Treba li mi dozvola?** treb-a lee mee dozvol-ah

*Men use the first alternative, women the second

Asking if things are allowed

ESSENTIAL INFORMATION

- May one smoke here?
  May we smoke here?
  May I smoke here?   **Može li se pušiti ovdje?**
  Can one smoke here?
  Can we smoke here?
  Can I smoke here?

- All these English variations can be expressed in one way in Serbo-Croat. To save space, only the first English version: May one . . .? is shown below.

WHAT TO SAY

Excuse me, please	**Izvinite molim**
	eez-veen-eet-eh mol-im
May one . . .	**Može li se . . .**
	mosh-eh lee seh . . .
camp here?	**kampovati ovdje?**
	kampov-atee ovd-yeh
come in?	**ući?**
	oochee
dance here?	**plesati ovdje?**
	ples-atee ovd-yeh
fish here?	**pecati ovdje?**
	ped-atee ov-d-yeh
get a drink here?	**dobiti piće ovdje?**
	dob-eetee peecheh ovd-yeh
get out this way?	**izaći ovim putem**
	eez-achee ov-im poot-em
get something to eat here?	**dobiti nešto za jesti ovdje?**
	dob-etee nesh-to za yes-tee ov-dyeh
leave one's thing here?	**ostaviti svoje stvari ovdje?**
	ostav-eetee svoyeh stva-ree ovd-yeh
look around?	**pogledati okolo?**
	pogleh-da-tee o-kolo
park here?	**parkirati ovdje?**
	parkeer-atee ovd-yeh

May one . . .	Može li se . . .
	mosh-eh lee seh . . .
sit here?	sjesti ovdje?
	s-yestee ovd-yeh
smoke here?	pušiti ovdje?
	poosh-eetee ovd-yeh
swim here?	plivati ovdje
	pleev-atee ovd-yeh
take photos here?	slikati ovdje?
	sleeka-tee ovd-yeh
telephone here?	telefonirati ovdje?
	telephon-eeratee ovd-yeh
wait here?	čekati ovdje?
	check-atee ovd-yeh

LIKELY REACTIONS

Yes, certainly	Da, sigurno
	da seeg-oornoh
Help yourself	Služite se
	sloosh-eeteh seh
I think so	Mislim da je tako
	mis-lim da yeh ta-ko
Of course	Sigurno
	seeg-oorno
Yes, but be careful	Da, ali pazite se
	da ah-lee paz-eeteh seh
No, certainly not	Ne, stvarno ne
	neh stvarno neh
I don't think so	Ne mislim da je tako
	neh mis-lim da yeh ta-ko
Not normally	Obično ne
	obeech-no neh
Sorry	Žao mi je
	sha-o mee yeh

Reference

PUBLIC NOTICES

● Key words on signs for drivers, pedestrians, travellers, shoppers and overnight guests.

AUTOPUT	Motorway
BAR	Bar
BESPLATAN ULAZ	Admission free
BIFE	Buffet
BOLNICA	Hospital
CARINARNICA	Customs
CESTARINA	Toll
ČEKAJ	Wait
ČEKAONICA	Waiting room
ČUVAJ SE PSA	Beware of the dog
DAME	Ladies
DOLAZAK	Arrivals
DOZVOLJENO PUŠITI	Smoking allowed
DRŽI SE NA DESNO	Keep right
DVOSMJERAN PROMET	Two way traffic
GARDEROBA	Left luggage
GOSPODA	Gentlemen
GURAJ	Push
HLADNO	Cold
IZDAJE SE SOBA	Room to let
IZGUBLJENE STVARI	Lost property
IZLAZ	Exit
IZLAZ (AUTOPUTA)	Exit (from motorway)
IZLAZ ZA NUŽDU	Emergency exit
IZNAJMIVA SE	To let
IZRAVAN PROMET	Through traffic
JEDAN SMJER	One way (street)
KASA (BLAGAJNA)	Cash desk
KAT (PRVI, DRUGI, TREĆI, PRIZEMLJE, PODRUM)	Floor (first, second, third, ground, basement)
KLIZOVITO	Slippery surface (road)
KRAJ (AUTOPUTA)	End (motorway)
KRAJ ZABRANE	End of parking restrictions
KUCAJ	Knock (door)
KUPAONICA	Bathroom
LAVINA	Avalanche area
LIFT	Lift

MEKANI RUBOVI	Soft verges
MILICIJA	Police
NA PRODAJU	For sale
NE DIRAJ	Do not touch
NEMA PRAZNO	No vacancies
NIJE PITKO	Not for drinking
NOSAČ (PORTIR)	Porter (hotels)
FAKIN	Porter (stations, ports)
ODLAZAK	Departures
ODRON KAMENA	Falling stones
OGRANIČENA BRZINA	Speed limit
OPASNO	Danger
OPASNA KRIVINA	Dangerous bend
OTVORENO	Open
OTVORENO OD . . . DO	Open from . . . to
PARKIRANJE	Car park
PARKIRANJE OGRANIČENO	Restricted parking
PAZI NA VLAK	Beware of the trains
PAZI/OPREZNO	Caution
PERON	Platform
PITKA VODA	Drinking water
PJEŠACI	Pedestrians
POČETAK AUTOPUTA	Start (motorway)
PODZEMAN PROLAZ	Subway
PODZEMNA ZELJEZNICA	Underground (train)
POMIČNE STEPENICE	Escalator
POPUST	Special offer
POTREBAN DISK ZA PARKIRANJE	Parking discs required
POVRŠINA POKVARENA	Bad surface (road)
PRAZNO	Vacant
PREDNOST NA DESNO	Priority to the right
PREKO PRUGE	Level crossing
PREPUSTI	Give way
PRIJEĆI	Crossroads
PRIJELAZ ZA BICIKLE	Cycle crossing
PRIVATNO	Private
PRODAJA KARATA	Ticket office
PROLAZ ZABRANJEN POD PRETNJOM GLOBE	Trespassers will be prosecuted
PROMETNA SVIJETLA (SEMAFOR)	Traffic lights
PROSTOR ZA STAJANJE	Standing room

PUT SE SUŽAVA	Road narrows
PUT ZA BICIKLE	Cycle path
RADOVI NA PUTU	Roadworks
RASKRSNICA	Crossroads
RASPRODAJA	Sale
RECEPCIJA	Reception
REZERVACIJA	Reservations
REZERVIRANO	Reserved
SAMOPOSLUGA	Self-service
ŠKOLA	School
SKRETANJE	Diversion
ŠKRIPAC	Cul-de-sac
STOJ	Halt/stop
SVIJETLA	Lights on
TOALETA	Toilet
TOPLO	Hot (tap)
TRPEZARIJA	Dining room
TUŠ	Shower
UDJI U TRAKU	Get in lane
ULAZ	Entrance
UPUTI	Guide
URED ZA INFORMACIJE	Information office
USPORAVAJ	Slow down
VAGON RESTORAN	Dining car
VELIKI NAGIB	Steep hill
VISOKI NAPON	High voltage
VLAK	Train
VOZI	Go
VOZI POLAGANO	Drive slowly
VUCI	Pull
ZA AUTOBUSE (SAMO)	For buses (only)
ZA TEŠKA KOLA	For heavy vehicles
ZA UNAJMITI	For hire
ZABRANJEN ULAZ	No admittance
ZABRANJENO	Forbidden
ZABRANJENO DIRATI	Do not touch
ZABRANJENO PARKIRANJE	No parking
ZABRANJENO PRETICANJE	Overtaking forbidden
ZABRANJENO PUŠITI	No smoking
ZABRANJENO SKRETANJE	No turning
ZATVORENO	Closed
ZATVORENO NEDJELJOM	Closed on Sundays
ZAUZETO	Engaged/occupied

ABBREVIATIONS

br	broj	number
Din	dinar	dinar
Dbk	Dubrovnik	Dubrovnik
gosp	gospodin	Mr
gdja	gospodja	Mrs
gdjica	gospodjica	Miss
god	godina	year
H	hladno	cold
h-s	hrvatsko-srpski	Croat-Serbian
itd	i tako dalje	etcetera
jedn	jednina	singular
mn	množina	plural
mr	muški rod	masculine gender
og	ove godine	this year
om	ovog mjeseca	this month
os	ove sedmice	this week
raz	razred	class
rkt	rimokatolik	Roman Catholic
SFRJ	Socijalistička Federativna Republika Jugoslavije	Socialist Federal Republic of Yugoslavia
SR	Socijalistička Republika	Socialist Republic
s-h	srpsko-hrvatski	Serbo-Croat
tel	telefon	telephone
tj	to jest	that is to say
ul	ulica	street
žr	ženski rod	feminine gender
adr	adresa	address
T	toplo	hot
trg	trgovina	trade
l	litar	litre
m	metar	metre
kg	kilogram	kilogram
pod	poduzeće	company
g	gram	gram
cm	centimetar	centimetre
km	kilometar	kilometre
kw	kilovat	kilowatt
£	funta	pound
SUP	Sekretaritjat Unutrašnjlh Poslova	Home Office

Ž	**Jugoslavenska Željeznica**	Yugoslav railways
MSJ	**Automoto Savez**	Yugoslavia Automobile
	Jugoslavije	Association
v	**sveti**	saint

NUMBERS

Cardinal numbers

0	**nula**	noolah
1	**jedan**	yed-an
2	**dva**	dva
3	**tri**	tree
4	**četiri**	chet-eeree
5	**pet**	peht
6	**šest**	shehst
7	**sedam**	seh-dam
8	**osam**	osam
9	**devet**	deh-vet
10	**deset**	deh-set
11	**jedanaest**	yeh-da-na-est
12	**dvanaest**	dvah-na-est
13	**trinaest**	tree-na-est
14	**četrnaest**	chet-er-na-est
15	**petnaest**	peht-na-est
16	**šesnaest**	shehst-na-est
17	**sedamnaest**	seh-dam-na-est
18	**osamnaest**	o-sam-na-est
19	**devetnaest**	deh-vet-na-est
20	**dvadeset**	dva-deh-set
21	**dvadeset jedan**	dva-deh-set yed-an
22	**dvadeset dva**	dva-deh-set dva
23	**dvadeset tri**	dva-deh-set tree
24	**dvadeset četiri**	dva-deh-set chet-eeree
25	**dvadeset pet**	dva-deh-set peht
26	**dvadeset šest**	dva-deh-seh shehst
27	**dvadeset sedam**	dva-deh-set seh-dam
28	**dvadeset osam**	dva-deh-set o-sam
29	**dvadeset devet**	dva-deh-set deh-vet
30	**trideset**	tree-deh-set
31	**trideset jedan**	tree-deh-setyed-an
32	**trideset dva**	tree-des-set dva

40	četrdeset	chet-er-deh-set
41	četrdeset jedan	chet-er-deh-set yed-an
42	četrdeset dva	chet-er-deh-set dva
50	pedeset	peh-deh-set
51	pedeset jedan	peh-deh-set yed-an
52	pedeset dva	peh-deh-set dva
60	šezdeset	shehz-deh-set
61	šezdeset jedan	shehz-deh-set yed-an
62	šezdeset dva	shehz-deh-set dva
70	sedamdeset	seh-dam-deh-set
71	sedamdeset jedan	seh-dam-deh-set yed-an
72	sedamdeset dva	seh-dam-deh-set dva
80	osamdeset	o-sam-deh-set
81	osamdeset jedan	o-sam-deh-set yed-an
82	osamdeset dva	o-sam-deh-set dva
90	devedeset	deh-vet-deh-set
91	devedeset jedan	deh-vet-deh-set yed-an
92	devedeset dva	deh-vet-deh-set dva
100	sto	sto
101	sto jedan	sto yed-an
110	sto deset	sto deh-set
120	sto dvadeset	sto dva-deh-set
200	dvjesta	dvee-yeh-sta
300	trista	tree-sta
400	cetrsto	chet-er-sto
500	petsto	peht-sto
600	šesto	sheh-sto
700	sedamsto	seh-dam-sto
800	osamsto	o-sam-sto
900	devetsto	deh-vet-sto
1,000	hiljada/tisuća	heel-ya-da/tees-oocha
2,000	dvije hiljade	dvee-yeh heel-ya-deh
3,000	tri hiljade	tree heel-ya-deh
10,000	deset hiljada	deh-set heel-yada
100,000	sto hiljada	sto heel-ya-da
1,000,000	milijun	meelee-yoon

Ordinal numbers

1st	prvi	per-vee
2nd	drugi	droo-ghee
3rd	treći	trechee
4th	četvrti	chet-ver-tee
5th	peti	peh-tee
6th	šesti	shes-tee
7th	sedmi	sed-mee
8th	osmi	os-mee
9th	deveti	deh-veh-tee
10th	deseti	deh-seh-tee
11th	jedanaesti	yed-ana-estee
12th	dvanaesti	dva-na-estee

TIME

What time is it?	**Koliko je sati?**
	kol-eeko yeh sa-tee
It's . . . (this is not translated in Serbo-Croat)	
one o'clock	**jedan sat**
	yed-an sat
two o'clock	**dva sata**
	dva sa-ta
three o'clock	**tri sata**
	tree sa-ta
four o'clock	**četiri sata**
	chet-eeree sa-ta
in the morning	**u jutro**
	oo yoo-tro
in the afternoon	**poslije podne**
	poslee-veh pod-neh
in the evening	**u veče**
	oo veh-cheh
at night	**noću**
	no-choo
It's . . . (this is not translated in Serbo-Croat)	
noon	**podne**
	pod-neh
midnight	**ponoć**
	po-noch
It's . . . (this is not translated in Serbo-Croat)	
five past five	**pet i pet**
	peht ee peht
ten past five	**pet i deset**
	peht ee deh-set
a quarter past five	**pet i petnaest**
	peht ee peht-na-est
twenty past five	**pet i dvadeset**
	peht ee dva-deh set
twenty-five past five	**pet i dvadeset pet**
	peht ee dva-deh-set peht
half past five	**pola šest**
	po-la shehst
twenty-five to six	**dvadeset pet do šest**
	dva-deh-set peht doh shehst
twenty to six	**dvadeset do šest**
	dva-deh-set doh shehst

a quarter to six	**petnaest do šest** peht-na-est doh shehst
ten to six	**deset do šest** deh-set doh shehst
five to six	**pet do šest** peht doh shehst
At what time . . . (does the train leave)?	**U koliko sato . . . (odlazi voz za)?** oo kol-eeko sa-tee . . . (odlaz-ee voz za)
At . . .	**U. . .** oo . . .
13.00	**trinaest (sati)** tree-na-est (sa-tee)
14.05	**četrnaest i pet** chet-er-na-est ee peht
15.10	**petnaest i deset** peht-na-est ee deh-set
16.15	**šesnaest i petnaest** shehst-na-est ee peht-na-est
17.20	**sedamnaest i dvadeset** seh-dam-na-est ee dva-deh-set
18.25	**osamnaest i dvadeset pet** o-sam-na-est ee dva-deh-set peht
19.30	**devetnaest i trideset** deh-vet-na-est ee tree-deh-set
20.35	**dvadeset i trideset pet** dva-deh-set ee tree-deh-set peht
21.40	**dvadeset jedan i četrdeset** dva-deh-set yed-an ee chet-er-deh-set
22.45	**dvadeset dva i cetrdeset pet** dva-deh-set dvah ee chet-er-deh-set peht
23.50	**dvadeset tri i pedeset** dva-deh-set tree ee peht-deh-set
0.55	**nula pedeset pet** noola peht-deh-set peht
in ten minutes	**za deset minuta** za deh-set meen-oota
in a quarter of an hour	**za petnaest minuta** za peht-na-est meen-oota
in half an hour	**za pola sata** za po-la sa-ta
in three quarters of an hour	**za četrdeset pet minuta** za chet-er-deh-set peht meen-oota

DAYS

Monday	**ponedjeljak**
	poned-yel-yak
Tuesday	**utorak**
	ooto-rak
Wednesday	**srijeda**
	sree-yeda
Thursday	**četvrtak**
	chet-ver-tak
Friday	**petak**
	peh-tak
Saturday	**subota**
	soo-bota
Sunday	**nedjelja**
	ned-yel-ya
last Monday	**prošli ponedjeljak**
	prosh-lee poned-yel-yak
next Tuesday	**sljedeći utorak**
	sleeyeh-deh-chee ootorak
on Wednesday	**u srijedu**
	oo sree-yedoo
on Thursday	**u četvrtak**
	oo chet-ver-tak
until Friday	**do petka**
	doh peht-ka
before Saturday	**prije subote**
	pree-yeh sooboteh
after Sunday	**poslije nedjelje**
	pos-lee-yeh ned-yel-yeh
the day before yesterday	**prekjučer**
	prek-yoo-cher
two days ago	**pred dva dana**
	pred dva da-na
yesterday	**jučer**
	yoo-cher
yesterday morning	**jučer u jutro**
	yoo-cher oo yoo-tro
yesterday afternoon	**jučer poslije podne**
	yoo-cher pos-lee-yeh pod-ne
last night	**sinoč**
	see-noch

oday	**danas**
	d*an*-us
his morning	**jutros**
	y*oo*t-ros
his afternoon	**danas poslije podne**
	d*an*-us pos-lee-yeh p*od*-neh
onight	**večeras**
	vech-*ai*ras
omorrow	**sutra**
	s*oo*tra
omorrow morning	**sutra u jutro**
	s*oo*tra oo y*oo*-tro
omorrow afternoon	**sutra poslije podne**
	s*oo*tra pos-lee-yeh p*od*-neh
omorrow evening	**sutra u veče**
	s*oo*tra oo v*e*cheh
omorrow night	**sutra noću**
	s*oo*tra n*o*choo
he day after tomorrow	**prekosutra**
	prek*o*-sootra

MONTHS AND DATES

anuary	**januar**
	y*a*-noo-ar
ebruary	**februar**
	feh-broo-ar
March	**mart**
	m*a*rt
April	**april**
	*a*p-reel
May	**maj**
	m*a*-ee
une	**juni**
	y*oo*-nee
uly	**juli**
	y*oo*-lee
August	**august**
	ah-oo-goost
eptember	**septembar**
	sep-t*e*m-bar

October	**oktobar**
	okto-bar
November	**novembar**
	novem-bar
December	**decembar**
	deh-tsem-bar
in January	**u januaru**
	oo ya-noo-ah-roo
until February	**do februara**
	doh feh-broo-ah-ra
before March	**prije marta**
	pree-yeh mar-ta
after April	**poslije aprila**
	pos-lee-yeh ap-reela'
during May	**kroz maj**
	kroz ma-ee
not until June	**ne do juna**
	neh doh yoo-na
the beginning of July	**početkom jula**
	pocket-kom yoo-la
the middle of August	**polovinom augusta**
	polo-veen-om ah-oo-goos-ta
the end of September	**svršetkom septembra**
	sver-shet-kom sep-tem-bra
last month	**prošli mjesec**
	prosh-lee m-yes-ets
this month	**ovaj mjesec**
	ov-aee m-yes-ets
next month	**slijedeči mjesec**
	slee-yed-echee m-yes-ets
in spring	**u prolječe**
	oo prol-yeh-cheh
in summer	**ljeti**
	l-yeh-tee
in autumn	**u jesen**
	oo yeh-sen
in winter	**zimi**
	zeemee
this year	**ove godine**
	ov-eh god-eeneh
last year	**prošle godine**
	prosh-leh god-eeneh

next year	**slijedeče godine**	
	slee-yed-echeh god-eeneh	
n 1982	**hiljadu devet sto osamdeset druge godine**	
	heel-ya-doo deh-vet sto osam-deh-set droogheh god-eeneh	
n 1985	**hiljadu devet sto osamdeset pete godine**	
	heel-ya-doo deh-vet sto osam-deh-set peh-teh god-eeneh	
n 1990	**hiljadu devet sto devedesete godine**	
	heel-ya-doo deh-vet sto deh-vet-deh-set-eh god-eeneh	
What's the date today?	**Koji je datum danas?**	
	koyee yeh da-toom dan-us	
It's the 6th of March	**Šesti mart**	
	sheh-stee mart	
It's the 12th of April	**Dvanaesti april**	
	dva-na-estee ap-reel	
It's the 21st of August	**Dvadeset prvi august**	
	dvadeh-set 'er-vee ow-goost	

Public holidays

Offices, shops and schools are all closed on the following dates.

1–2 January	**Nova godina**	New Year holiday
1–2 May	**Prvi Maj**	Labour Day
4 July	**Dan borca**	Fighter's Day
29–30 November	**Dan Republike**	Days of the Republic

Republican national holidays

Serbia 7 July
Montenegro 13 July
Slovenia 22 July
Croatia, Bosnia and Herzegovina 27 July
Macedonia 2 August and 11 October

COUNTRIES AND NATIONALITIES

Countries

Albania	**Albanija**
	*a*lba-nee-ya
Australia	**Australija**
	ah-oo-stral-ya
Austria	**Austrija**
	ah-oo-stri-ya
Belgium	**Belgija**
	b*e*l-ghee-ya
Britain	**Britanija**
	br*ee*tan-eeya
Canada	**Kanada**
	ka-nah-da
East Africa	**Istočna Afrika**
	*ee*stoch-na *a*frika
East Germany	**Istočna Nijemačka**
	*ee*st-ochna nee-yeh-mach-ka
Eire	**Irska**
	*ee*r-ska
England	**Engleska**
	*e*n-gl*e*ska
France	**Francuska**
	fr*a*n-tsoo-ska
Greece	**Grčka**
	g*e*rch-ka
Hungary	**Madjarska**
	m*a*h-jar-ska
India	**Indija**
	*i*ndee-ya
Italy	**Italija**
	*i*talee-ya
Luxembourg	**Luksemburg**
	l*oo*x-em-boorg
Netherlands	**Nizozemska**
	n*ee*zo-zemska
New Zealand	**Novi Zeland**
	n*o*vee z*e*hland
Northern Ireland	**Sjeverna Irska**
	s-yev-airna *ee*r-ska

Pakistan	**Pakistan**
	pak-eestan
Portugal	**Portugal**
	port-oogal
Romania	**Rumunija**
	roo-moo-nee-ya
Scotland	**Škotska**
	sh-kot-ska
South Africa	**Južna Afrika**
	yoosh-na afrika
Spain	**Španija**
	shpanee-ya
Switzerland	**Švicarska**
	shvi-tsar-ska
United States	**Amerika**
	amerika
USSR	**Rusija**
	roosee-ya
Wales	**Vels**
	vehls
West Germany	**Zapadna Njemačka**
	zap-adna nee-eh-mach-ka
West Indies	**Karibi**
	karee-bee
Yugoslavia	**Jugoslavija**
	yoogoslav-eeya

Nationalities

[Use the first alternative for men, the second for women]

Albanian	**Albanac/Albanka**
	alba-nats/alban-ka
American	**Amerikanac/Amerikanka**
	amerik-an-ats/amerikanka
Australian	**Australac/Australjka**
	ah-oo-stral-ats/ah-oo-stral-ka
Canadian	**Kanadjanin/Kanadjanka**
	kanaj-aneen/kanaj-anka
East African	**Istočni Afrikanac/Istočna afrikanka**
	eest-och-nee afrikan-ats/eestoch-na afrikanka
East German	**Istočni Nijemac/Istočna Nijemica**
	eest-och-nee nee-yeh-mats/ eest-och-na nee-yeh-meetsa
English	**Englez/Engleskinja**
	en-glez/englez-skeen-ya
Hungarian	**Madjar/Madjarica**
	mah-jar/mah-jar-eetsa
Indian	**Indus/Induskinja**
	indoos/indoos-keen-ya
Irish	**Irac/Irkinja**
	eerats/eerkeen-ya
New Zealander	**Novo Zelandez/Novo Zeladjanka**
	novo zel-andez/novo zelaj-anka
Pakistani	**Pakistanac/Pakistanka**
	pakeestan-ats/pakeestanka
Romanian	**Rumun/Rumunjka**
	roo-moon/roo-moon-ka
Russian	**Rus/Ruskinja**
	roos/roos-keen-ya
Scots	**Škot/Škotkinja**
	shkot/shkot-keen-ya
South African	**Južni Afrikanac/Južna Afrikanka**
	yoosh-nee afrikan-ats/yoosh-na afrikanka
Welsh	**Velšanin/Velšanka**
	velsh-anin/velshanka
West Indian	**Iz Kariba**
	eez karee-ba
Yugoslav	**Jugoslaven/Jugoslavenka**
	yoogoslaven/yoogoslav-enka

DEPARTMENT STORE GUIDE

Alati	Tools
Auto oprema	Car accessories
Blagajna	Cash
Bluze	Blouses
Brodska oprema	Boat accessories
Čarape	Stockings
Četvrti	Fourth
Ćilimi	Carpets
Darovi	Gifts
Dječje igračke	Toys
Dragulji	Jewellery
Drugi	Second (floor)
Donje rublje	Underclothes
Donje rublje za dame	Underwear (women)
Električni aparati	Electrical appliances
Fotografia	Photography
Frizerski salon	Hairdresser
Gramofonske ploče	Records
Grudnjaci	Bras
Gvoždje	Laminates
Hrana	Food
Informacije	Information
Jastuci	Cushions
Kamping	Camping
Kamp oprema	Camping requisites
Keramika	Ceramics
Knjige	Books
Konfekcijska odjeća	Ready-made clothing
Kozmetika	Cosmetics
Kožna galanterija	Leather goods
Kravate	Ties
Kristal	Crystal
Krojački pribor	Haberdashery
Kućni namještaj	Home furnishings
Kuhinjski namještaj	Kitchen furniture
Moda za dame	Ladies fashion
Obuća	Shoes
Odio košulja	Shirt department
Oprema za novorodjenče	Layette
Papirnica	Stationery
Parfumerija	Perfumery
Pisaće potrebštine	Stationery

Podrum	Basement
Pojasi	Belts
Pokrivači	Blankets
Pokućstvo	Furniture
Porculan	China
Posteljina	Bedding
Posudje	Crockery
Prizemlje	Ground (floor)
Prvi	First (floor)
Puloveri	Pullovers
Pušenje zabranjeno	No smoking
Radio aparati	Radios
Ribo-materijal	Fishing gear
Rublje	Linen
Sanitarije	Bathroom requisites
Satovi	Watches – clocks
Suveniri	Souvenirs
Kat	Floor
Sredstva za čišćenje	Cleaning materials
Staklarija	Glassware
Steznici	Girdles
Sve za putovanje	Travel articles
Šeširi	Millinery
Štofovi	Materials/fabrics
Televizija	Television
Tekstil za kuću	Furnishing fabrics
Treći	Third (floor)
'Uradi-sam' (za hobiste)	Do-it-yourself
Za damu/za dame	Ladieswear
Za djecu	Child
Za muškarce	Menswear
Zastori/zavjesi	Curtains
Zemljano sudje	Earthenware
Željeznarija	Hardware

CONVERSION TABLES

Read the centre column of these tables from right to left to convert
from metric to imperial and from left to right to convert from
imperial to metric e.g. 5 litres = 8.80 pints; 5 pints = 2.84 litres

pints		litres		gallons		litres
1.76	1	0.57		0.22	1	4.55
3.52	2	1.14		0.44	2	9.09
5.28	3	1.70		0.66	3	13.64
7.07	4	2.27		0.88	4	18.18
8.80	5	2.84		1.00	5	22.73
10.56	6	3.41		1.32	6	27.28
12.32	7	3.98		1.54	7	31.82
14.08	8	4.55		1.76	8	36.37
15.84	9	5.11		1.98	9	40.91

ounces		grams		pounds		kilos
0.04	1	28.35		2.20	1	0.45
0.07	2	56.70		4.41	2	0.91
0.11	3	85.05		6.61	3	1.36
0.14	4	113.40		8.82	4	1.81
0.18	5	141.75		11.02	5	2.27
0.21	6	170.10		13.23	6	2.72
0.25	7	198.45		15.43	7	3.18
0.28	8	226.80		17.64	8	3.63
0.32	9	255.15		19.84	9	4.08

inches		centimetres		yards		metres
0.39	1	2.54		1.09	1	0.91
0.79	2	5.08		2.19	2	1.83
1.18	3	7.62		3.28	3	2.74
1.58	4	10.16		4.37	4	3.66
1.95	5	12.70		5.47	5	4.57
2.36	6	15.24		6.56	6	5.49
2.76	7	17.78		7.66	7	6.40
3.15	8	20.32		8.65	8	7.32
3.54	9	22.86		9.84	9	8.23

miles		kilometres
0.62	1	1.61
1.24	2	3.22
1.86	3	4.83
2.49	4	6.44
3.11	5	8.05
3.73	6	9.66
4.35	7	11.27
4.97	8	12.87
5.59	9	14.48

A quick way to convert kilometres to miles: divide by 8 and multiply by 5. To convert miles to kilometres: divide by 5 and multiply by 8.

fahrenheit (°F)	centigrade (°C)		lbs/ sq in	k/ sq cm
212°	100°	boiling point	18	1.3
100°	38°		20	1.4
98.4°	36.9°	body temperature	22	1.5
86°	30°		25	1.7
77°	25°		29	2.0
68°	20°		32	2.3
59°	15°		35	2.5
50°	10°		36	2.5
41°	5°		39	2.7
32°	0°	freezing point	40	2.8
14°	−10°		43	3.0
−4°	−20°		45	3.2
			46	3.2
			50	3.5
			60	4.2

To convert °C to °F, divide by 5, multiply by 9 and add 32. To convert °F to °C, take away 32, divide by 9 and multiply by 5.

CLOTHING SIZES

Remember – always try on clothes before buying.
Clothing sizes are usually unreliable.

women's dresses and suits

Europe	38	40	42	44	46	48
UK	32	34	36	38	40	42
USA	10	12	14	16	18	20

men's suits and coats

Europe	46	48	50	52	54	56
UK and USA	36	38	40	42	44	46

men's shirts

Europe	36	37	38	39	41	42	43
UK and USA	14	14½	15	15½	16	16½	17

socks

Europe	38–39	39–40	40–41	41–42	42–43
UK and USA	9½	10	10½	11	11½

shoes

Europe	34	35½	36½	38	39	41	42	43	44	45
UK	2	3	4	5	6	7	8	9	10	11
USA	3½	4½	5½	6½	7½	8½	9½	10½	11½	12½

Do it yourself

Some notes on the language

This section does not deal with 'Grammar' as such. The purpose here is to explain some of the most obvious and elementary nuts and bolts of the language, based on the principal phrases included in the book. This information should enable you to produce numerous sentences of your own making.

There is no pronunciation guide in most of this section, partly because it would get in the way of the explanations and partly because you have to do it yourself at this stage if you are serious – work out the pronunciation from all the earlier examples in the book.

NOUNS

All nouns in Serbo-Croat belong to one of three genders: masculine, feminine or neuter, irrespective of whether they refer to living things or inanimate object.

As in many other languages, Serbo-Croat nouns have different forms according to their *gender* (masculine, feminine or neuter) and to their *number* (singular or plural). However, unlike some well-known European languages (French, Spanish, Italian) they also change according to their function in the sentence (subject, object, etc.) i.e. according to their *case*. There are seven cases in Serbo-Croat.

Does getting these different forms correct matter? Not unless you want to make a serious attempt to speak correctly and scratch beneath the surface of the language. You would probably be understood if you use the wrong form providing your pronunciation was good.

In order to practise the basic phrases used in this section only *two* cases will be introduced.

Singular nouns

	masculine	feminine	neuter
the/an address		adresa	
the/an apple		jabuka	
the/a bill	račun		
the/a bottle of wine		boca vina	
the/a chicken			pile
the/a cup of tea		šalica čaja	
the/an egg			jaje
the/a glass of beer	čaša piva		
the/a key	ključ		
the/a menu	jelovnik		
the/a receipt		priznanica	
the/a room		soba	
the/a sandwich	sendvič		
the/a suitcase	kofer		
the/a timetable	red		

Important things to remember

- You can often tell if a noun is masculine, feminine or neuter by its ending. When they are the subject of a sentence (Nominative Case), masculine nouns in the singular usually end in a consonant, feminine nouns in **-a** and neuter nouns in **-e** or **-o**. Look at the examples in the table above.

- No word is used normally for *the, a, some* or *any* in Serbo Croat. If we take as an English example *Where is the suitcase?*, the Serbo-Croat translation **Gdje je kofer?** would mean literally *Where is suitcase?* Similarly, *Have you got any coffee?* would translate as **Imate li kavu?**, literally *Have you got coffee?* You can guess whether you would say *a* or *the* etc. in English from the context of the sentence. However, if you wish to specify the quantity *I'll have a (one) doughnut* you can use **jedan** (*one*): **Htio/htjela bih jedan krafen.**

- ! Caution

  In phrases beginning: I'll have . . .

  Have you got . . .?

  I'd like . . .

  Where can I get . . .?

Serbo-Croat nouns become the object of the sentence (called the Accusative Case) and the endings of the *feminine* singular noun change from **-a** to **-u**, e.g. **adresa** becomes **adresu**.

Practice saying and writing these sentences in Serbo-Croat. Watch for the caution sign (!) and note that *I'd like/I'll have* change their construction according to whether you are a man (**želio/htio**) or a woman (**željela/htjela**). You will have seen examples of this throughout the phrase book.

Where is the key?	**Gdje je ključ**
Where is the suitcase?	**Gdje je . . .?**
Where is the address?	**. . .**
Have you got the timetable?	**Imate li red?**
Have you got the address?	**Imate li . . .?**
Have you got the menu?	**. . .**
I'd like a glass of beer	**Želio/željela bih čašu piva**

(Note that **piva** 'of beer' and later **čaja** 'of tea' and **vina** 'of wine' do not change their endings.)

I'd like the bill	**Želio/željela bih . . .**
I'd like an apple	**. . .**
I'd like the receipt	**. . .**
Where can I get a cup of tea?	**Gdje mogu dobiti šalicu čaja?**
Where can I get the key?	**Gdje mogu dobiti . . . ?**
Where can I get a room?	**. . .**
I'll have a bottle of wine	**Htio/htjela bih bocu vina**
I'll have a glass of beer	**Htio/htjela bih . . .**
I'll have the chicken	**. . .**

Now make up more sentences along the same lines. Try adding please: **molim** at the beginning or the end.

Note that if you just want to ask for:

A glass of beer, please	**Čašu piva, molim**

The noun 'a glass' must be in the Accusative Case because the phrase *I'd like* or *I'll have* is understood although not said.

Now practise plural nouns on the next page.

Plural nouns

Look at the table below; note that some of the examples don't follow the basic rule (see 'Important things to remember' below) and need to be memorized.

	masculine	feminine	neuter
addresses		adrese	
apples		jabuke	
bills	računi		
bottles of wine		boce vina	
chickens			pilići
cups of tea		šalice čaja	
eggs			jaja
glasses of beer		čaše piva	
keys	ključevi		
menus	jelovnici		
receipts		priznanice	
rooms		sobe	
sandwiches	sendviči		
suitcases	koferi		
timetables	redovi		

Important things to remember

- When they are the subject of the sentence (Nominative Case) most masculine nouns in the plural end in **-i**.
- Some masculine nouns of one syllable form the plural by adding **-evi** or **-ovi**, e.g. **ključ** becomes **ključevi** and **red** becomes **redovi**.
- Most feminine nouns end in **-e**.
- Most neuter nouns end in **-a**.
- ! Caution
  In phrases beginning:
  I'll have . . .
  Have you got . . . ?
  I'd like . . .
  Where can I get . . .?
  as in the singular, Serbo-Croat nouns become the object of the sentence (Accusative Case) but in the plural, the endings of *masculine* nouns change from **-i** to **-e,** e.g. **računi** becomes **račune**.

If a number is used with a plural noun e.g. *two* chickens, *five* children, the endings of the noun change according to *which* number! You will see examples of this throughout the book.

Practice saying and writing these sentences in Serbo-Croat. Watch for the caution sign (!) and remember that the words for *of wine/of beer/of tea* (**vina/piva/čaja**) always remains the same:

Where are the eggs?	**Gdje su jaja?**
Where are the suitcases?	**Gdje su . . .?**
Where are the bottles of wine?	**. . .**
Have you got any sandwiches?	**Imate li sendviče**
Have you got any rooms?	**Imate li . . .?**
Have you got the keys?	**. . .**
I'd like some apples	**Želio/željela bih . . .**
I'd like some eggs	**. . .**
Where can I get some bottles of wine?	**Gdje mogu dobiti . . .?**
Where can I get the keys?	**. . .**
Where can I get some suitcases?	**. . .**
I'll have the sandwiches	**Htio/htjela bih . . .**
I'll have the bottles of wine	**. . .**

THIS AND THAT

Use these two words in Serbo-Croat
ovo (this)
to (that)

If you don't know the Serbo-Croat name for an object, just point and say:

Htio/htjela bih ovo	I'll have this
Želio/željela bih to	I'd like that

Now study the verbs on the next page.

HELPING OTHERS

You can help yourself with such phrases as:

I'd like . . . the bill	**Želio/željela bih . . . račun**
Where can I get . . . a cup of tea?	**Gdje mogu dobiti . . . šalicu čaja?**
I'll have . . . a glass of beer	**Htio/htjela bih . . . čašu piva**

If you come across a compatriot having trouble making himself or herself understood, you should be able to speak to the Yugoslav person on their behalf. Note that *he, she, we* and *they* are not usually translated in Serbo-Croat. (A pronunciation guide is provided from here on.)

He'd like . . .	**Želio bi račun** shel-yoo bee rach-oon
She'd like . . .	**Željela bi račun** shel-yel-a bee rach-oon.
Where can he get . . .?	**Gdje može dobiti šalicu čaja?** gd-yeh mosh-eh dob-eetee shal-eetsoo cha-ya
Where can she get . . .?	**Gdje može dobiti šalicu čaja?** gd-yeh mosh-eh dob-eetee shal-eetsoo cha-ya
He'll have . . .	**Htio bi čašu piva** htee-o bee chash-oo peeva
She'll have . . .	**Htjela bi čašu piva** ht-yelah bee chash-oo peeva

You can also help a couple or a group if *they* are having difficulties

They'd like . . .	**Željeli bi račun** shel-yel-ee bee rach-roon
Where can they get . . .?	**Gdje mogu dobiti šalicu čaja?** gd-yeh mog-oo dob-eetee shal-eetsoo cha-ya
They'll have . . .	**Htjeli bi čašu piva** hty-elee bee chash-oo peeva

Index

Arthur Eperon
Travellers' Italy

A whole variety of holiday routes to guarantee that you eat, drink, explore and relax in the places the Italians themselves would choose. The best places to sample local speciality foods and wines, spectacular scenery, facts the history books won't tell you, as well as the magnificent beaches and art treasures you'd expect. Arthur Eperon is one of the best-known travel writers in Europe and has an extensive knowledge of Italy and its food and wine. With an introduction by Frank Bough.

Travellers' France

Six major routes across France, taking in the best restaurants and hotels, visiting the most interesting out-of-the-way places. This detailed and up-to-the-minute handbook is for the traveller who wants more out of France than a mad dash down the motorway. Each of the six routes across the country is illustrated with a specially-commissioned two-colour map, and includes a host of information on where to eat and drink, where to take children, where to stay, and how to get the most out of the towns and countryside.

Ken Welsh
Hitch-Hiker's Guide to Europe

The new and completely updated edition of this invaluable guide covers Europe, North Africa and the Middle East. Ken Welsh gives advice on routes to take, what to take, eating, sleeping, local transport, what to see, together with information on currency, useful phrases and working abroad.

'Hitch-hikers will adopt it as their travelling bible but it's amusing and informative for those who fancy more traditional ways' BBC

Companion Language Dictionaries

English – Français   French – Anglais
English – Deutsch   German – Englisch
English – Español   Spanish – Inglés
English – Italiano   Italian – Inglese

These pocket bilingual dictionaries have been especially designed for use by both English *and* French, German, Spanish and Italian speakers and are suitable for tourists, business travellers and students up to approximately O level. Each dictionary contains about 10,000 headwords; each entry contains a minimum of useful grammatical information such as gender of nouns, cases with German verbs etc. There is a pronunciation guide to both the foreign language and English headwords.

Harrap's New Pocket French and English Dictionary

The classic French/English and English/French reference for students and travellers, this edition contains some 4,500 entries in each language, including all the principal words in current use – recent additions to both languages, scientific terms, tourist expressions. Entries also contain phonetic renderings and examples of idiomatic use.

A Multilingual Commercial Dictionary

Some 3,000 words and phrases in common commercial use are listed in English, French, German, Spanish and Portuguese followed by their translation in the other languages. The equivalent American expression is also included where relevant. Simple to use and invaluable for everyday reference, the dictionary covers terms used throughout banking, accounting, insurance, shipping, export and import and international trade.

Pan Study Aids

Published jointly by Heinemann Educational Books and Pan Books

Pan Study Aids are a major new series developed to help school and college students prepare for examinations. All of the authors are experienced teachers/examiners at O level. School Certificate and equivalent examinations and authors of textbooks used in schools and colleges worldwide.

Each volume in the series:
- explains its subject and covers clearly and concisely and with excellent illustrations the essential points of the syllabus, drawing attention to common areas of difficulty and to areas which carry most marks in the exam
- gives guidance on how to plan revision, and prepare for the exam, outlining what examiners are looking for
- provides practice by including typical exam questions and exercises

French
C. Beswick and P. J. Downes

German
D. Shotter

Spanish
D. Utley

Other titles available: Physics, Chemistry, Maths, Biology, Human Biology, English Language, Geography 1 & 2, Economics, Commerce, Accounts and Book-keeping, British Government and Politics, History 1 & 2, Effective Study Skills

edited by Harriet Peacock
The Alternative Holiday Catalogue

If you're looking for a holiday that you won't find in a travel
agent's window . . . if there's something you've always wanted
to try your hand at . . . or if you want to take your special interest
on holiday with you, this A-to-Z of ideas and information is the
book you need. 150 different types of special-interest holiday,
from backgammon and Bible-study to Zen, upholstery and giving
up smoking. This book tells you where to go, what to take, what
it costs, and what you'll find when you get there.

John Slater
Just Off for the Weekend
Slater's hotel guide

The bestselling author of *Just Off the Motorway* has selected
more than a hundred places to stay, with details of what to see
and walks to take, specially recommended pubs and restaurants
– and all within a Friday evening's drive from one of England's big
cities. With an introduction by Anna Ford.

Just Off the Motorway

The new and enlarged edition of a sensational bestseller.
Introduction by Russell Harty

Here's the new, bang-up-to-date edition of the handbook
everyone needs. Detailed research, careful sampling, and more
than 150 maps show where you can find any service you require
– cheaper and better – by turning off at a junction and driving no
more than three miles off the motorway – eating, drinking,
overnight stops, breakdown services, petrol, visits.

'Worth a detour to buy it' DAILY MAIL

Ronald Ridout
The Pan Spelling Dictionary

The quick and easy guide to accurate spelling.
Clearly laid out, with brief and straightforward definitions
of 34,000 words. A supplement to the main text
identifies American spellings where they differ from
standard English. Also includes lists of proper names and
abbreviations, an outline of the main principles of English
spelling, and clear instructions for using the book to find the word
you want. Ideal for the home, the classroom or the office.